Spark the Brain, Ignite the Pen

Quick Writes for Kindergarten Through High School Teachers and Beyond

Second Edition

Spark the Brain, Ignite the Pen

Quick Writes for Kindergarten Through High School Teachers and Beyond

Second Edition

edited by

Samuel Totten
University of Arkansas, Fayetteville

Helen Eaton
Holcomb Elementary, Fayetteville, Arkansas

Shelley Dirst
Arkansas Department of Education,
Little Rock, Arkansas

Clare Lesieur
Eureka Springs Elementary,
Eureka Springs, Arkansas

Information Age Publishing, Inc.
Charlotte, North Carolina • www.infoagepub.com

Library of Congress Cataloging-in-Publication Data

Spark the brain, ignite the pen : quick writes for kindergarten through high school teachers and beyond / edited by Samuel Totten ... [et al.]. — 2nd ed.
    p. cm.
  Includes bibliographical references.
  ISBN 978-1-60752-087-0 (paperback) — ISBN 978-1-60752-088-7 (hardcover) 1. English language—Composition and exercises—Study and teaching. 2. Creative writing. I. Totten, Samuel.
  LB1576.S723 2009
  372.62'3—dc22

                                                                          2009006207

Printed in the United States of America.

Samuel Totten dedicates this book to James Gray, the founder of the National Writing Project; Jayne Marlink, my outstanding instructor during the Open at the University of California at Davis back in 1986; Joye Alberts, former codirector of the Oklahoma State University Writing Project at Stillwater, who introduced me to the concept of quick writes; and last but in no way least, all of the fine TCs in the Northwest Arkansas Writing Project who have energized me as I enter my 30th year in the field of education.

Helen Eaton dedicates this book to my writing inspiration, Laura Ingalls Wilder, who recorded ordinary events of everyday life with simple elegance; and to my friend and colleague Jeanne King, who taught me the value of choice and that creativity takes many forms.

Clare Lesieur dedicates this book to Janis Gibson for being a voice for literacy and steering me to NWAWP; to the 2000 Invitational gang, for 16 days I'll always remember; to Mary Wince, you are who I aspire to be as a teacher; to my Skyline friends, who make a difference for kids every day; and to my family, for your never-ending supply of love and raw material.

Shelley Dirst dedicates this book to Helen Eaton and Cheri Olmstead, the codirectors of the Northwest Arkansas Writing Project's Fayetteville Open Summer Writing Institute, for introducing me to both the National Writing Project and the concept of quick writes.

CONTENTS

Introduction xiii

ENGLISH LANGUAGE ARTS

Imagination **3**
  1. Got Warts? 3
  2. You Picked A Fine Time to Leave Me Lucille 4
  3. Wanted: An Heir for a $375,000 Estate 8
  4. "Bearly" Work 9
  5. A Picture Paints a Thousand Words 10

Lists **13**
  6. What I Know/Don't Know: In Search of Research Topics 13
  7. Are You More Like? 15
  8. Promises, Promises, Promises 17
  9. 100 Things to Do Before You Die! 19
 10. What's It Like to Wait? 21
 11. What Would You Do? 22
 12. Who Is an Expert? 25
 13. I Remember 27
 14. Heaven on Earth 29
 15. Darwin Awards! 32

Memories **35**
 16. The Truth Will Set You Free 35
 17. A Matter of Choice 36
 18. Even Sick Days Have Good Memories 37
 19. Have You Ever Had One of Those Days 38
 20. Ira Sleeps Over 38
 21. Dead Poet's Society 40

22. Any Great Aunts Out There? 41
23. A Most Unforgettable Character 42
24. Remembering Relatives 43
25. Dancing Memories 44
26. All the Places to Love 45
27. Treasured Treasures 46
28. Do You Speak My Language? 47
29. Remembering? 48
30. What is Your Literacy Autobiography? 49
31. Bowl After Bowl of Chicken Soup 50
32. Don't Worry, Be Happy 51

Self-Discovery **53**
33. What I Know 53
34. Art, Like Morality, Consists of Drawing
    the Line Somewhere! 55
35. A Gift From the Heart 56
36. Examining One's Life 57
37. It is All in the Eye of the Beholder 58
38. Living Life for All Its Worth 60
39. My Achilles' Heel 61
40. Introducing a New Me 62
41. What's Your Fortune? A Fun-Story Starter 63
42. Celebrations: "You're in Charge!" 64
43. Salt in His Shoes: Michael Jordan in Pursuit of a Dream 65
44. One Hit Wonder 66
45. Avocations 67
46. What Were You Afraid of? 69
47. Face Your Fears 70
48. Truer Words Have Never Been Spoken 71
49. "Sweet Dreams" 72
50. The Choice of Your Life 74

Writer's Craft **75**
51. Hats Off to You 75
52. "... And Another Thing" 77
53. Reading with "Author Glasses" On, or "Hey! I Could Do That!" ... 78
54. I Wanna: Persuasive Writing 79
55. Things Aren't Always What They Seem 80
56. I've Got the Blues 82
57. Poems for Two Voices 83
58. Word Poems and the Content Areas 85
59. CoCo's Voice 87
60. Have I Got a Story for You! 88
61. The Mysteries of Harris Burdick 90

62. How Lame! 91
63. Come Take a Free Write 93
64. Ridiculous Rhymes 94
65. Love Your Lemon 96
66. Hoot's Diner: Place with Personality 97
67. She Did WHAT? 99
68. Famous First Pages: A Syntax Study 100
69. "Round and Round We Go ..." 103
70. Into the Forest: Imitating the Writer's Craft 104
71. Do You Hear What I Hear? 105
72. Five Senses 106
73. When I Was Young in the Mountains 108
74. Photo Memories 109
75. Sweeter Than Kisses 110
76. Meanwhile, Back at the Ranch 112
77. "Schoolsville" 113
78. Get in the Picture 115
79. My Favorite Place 116
80. The Most Beautiful, Exciting, or Exotic Place I've Ever Been 117
81. My Town May Not Have "Big Shoulders,"
    But It Has What Chicago Can Only Dream Of 119
82. Why I Prefer... 120
83. How Creative Can You Get? Crazy, Mixed-Up Story Starters 122
84. Chasing Rainbows 123
85. From Mrs. Malaprop to Archie Bunker to....: Malapropisms 126
86. The Bite of Satire 127
87. For the Love of SPAM! 129

Ties to Literature **131**
88. Gift from the Heart 131
89. What? Me Scared? 132
90. Is "No Man an Island" or ...? 133
91. Machiavelli's Descendents 135
92. Stories for Bear: Launching the Reading
    and Writing Workshops 137
93. Famous First Lines 139
94. Dear Author 140

MATH

95. Talk Geometry to Me 143
96. What's Your Sign 146
97. Word Connections 147
98. Rubber Band Words 148

99. Triangle Personality 149
100. Vertex and Perimeter 150
101. A Diamond is for Reflecting 152
102. Number Personalities 154
103. Polygon Dialogue 155
104. Can You Build It? 156
105. Pattern Block Puzzles 161

SCIENCE AND TECHNOLOGY

106. Wii-Mote Magic 161
107. Listen to Your Body 162
108. How Can the Easter Bunny Lay Eggs? 163
109. Creating the World Anew 165
110. Creature Features 166
111. Here We Go 'Round 167
112. Shark or Dolphin? You Decide 169
113. What the World Be Like Without 170
114. Take a Haiku Hike! 171
115. Nature's Treasures 172
116. And Just Who's to Blame? 173
117. Take a Ride on the Magic School Bus 174
118. Seeing Through the Eyes of Another 175
119. Tell Me What's So Important 179
120. What Makes a Human Being Human? 182
121. What's Next? Extinguishing Our World? 183

SOCIAL STUDIES

122. Looking the Other Way: What's It Take to Be
     Our Brothers' and Sisters' Keeper? 189
123. "I'll Never Forget Where I Was When ..." 190
124. Capturing Personal, Local, National and
     International History in a Time Capsule 191
125. Power of the Pen 192
126. Radical Reactions 193
127. I'll Take You There 194
128. NIMBY or Not in My Back Yard 195
129. Double Meanings 196
130. Dinner for Two 198
131. The Simple Life 199
132. Immigration and You 200

133. Capturing the Essence of History: Writing Captions for
     Political Cartoons. 202
134. First Encounter 203
135. I, Too, Was There 204
136. I Dream of Going to 205
137. Civil Rights 206
138. What If? 207
139. Just a Lookin' for a Home 209
140. They Came Across the Sea 210
141. A Knight's Tale 211
142. Food Often Makes the Place 213
143. "It's Out There Somewhere, But Who Knows
     Where and Who Really Cares? 214
144. War Is 215
145. The Most Perfect Place in the Universe 215
146. Civil Disobedience 217
147. I'd Like to Get to Know You 218
148. One Wish to Make the World a Better Place 219

INTRODUCTION

Samuel Totten, Helen Eaton, Shelley Dirst, and Clare Lesieur

"Quick writes almost seem magical!" Those words were spoken by a veteran teacher taking part in a summer writing institute sponsored by the Northwest Arkansas Writing Project, an official site of the National Writing Project. Quick writes may seem magical, but they are not. In reality, a quick write is a simple but innovative way to incorporate prewriting into the classroom curriculum.

WHAT ARE QUICK WRITES?

A quick write is an on-demand, focused free-writing exercise written in response to a stimulating prompt. Its purpose is, in part, to promote student thinking and/or creativity. Quick writes engage students in ways that cause them to think first and write second. The stimulus sets the brain in motion. While the writing generated from a quick write may later be crafted into a polished piece, the intent of the original draft is not for evaluation.

To conduct a quick write activity, teachers provide students with a brief but highly engaging stimulus (e.g., a thought-provoking scenario or question; a provocative statement, a poem, song lyric, newspaper article, or

Spark the Brain, Ignite the Pen: Quick Writes for Kindergarten Through High School Teachers and Beyond, 2nd Edition, pp. xiii–xix
Copyright © 2009 by Information Age Publishing

story; a song that is likely to induce reflection or creative thinking, or an engaging movie clip) and directions as to how the students should respond in writing. The audience, form, purpose, and point of view may be specified or left open-ended. In certain cases, some students may want to create their own responses rather than stick to the prompt provided. Such freedom should be encouraged.

Ultimately, each student writes a short piece in the few minutes following the stimulus. The goal is not for students to complete a finished piece in the short time provided, but rather for students to rough out a draft. That said, it is remarkable how pieces developed in such a manner result in descriptive, witty, and/or insightful pieces.

Essentially, quick writes constitute one of the many types of prewriting exercises that can be used in conjunction with the writing process. In that regard, they help students to access prior knowledge and to focus their thinking. Through the use of quick writes, even the most reluctant writers are, more often than not, motivated to write. In many cases, they also gain confidence in their ability to tackle the blank page.

THE FOCUS OF THIS BOOK, AND THE
RATIONALE FOR A SECOND EDITION

The express purpose of *Spark the Brain, Ignite the Pen: Quick Writes for Kindergarten Through High School Teachers and Beyond* is to offer a variety of accessible and highly engaging writing activities developed and classroom-tested by teachers from all grade levels and content areas. Each of the contributors is a teacher consultant for the Northwest Arkansas Writing Project (NWAWP) based at the University of Arkansas, Fayetteville.

One of the many beauties of a quick write is that its use extends beyond the domain of the English teacher. In fact, many of the quick writes included herein may be used as-is or adapted for specific curricular purposes by a wide range of teachers. What's more, once teachers experiment with these activities, they quickly begin to see how to develop their own quick writes.

Due to the remarkable popularity of the first edition of *Spark the Brain, Ignite the Pen*, the coeditors almost immediately began to consider the possibility of expanding the book by including new quick writes by new teacher consultants (TCs) in NWAWP. Additionally, the coeditors decided that there was a need to add a much stronger section of quick writes that could be used for the express purpose of "writing to learn" within the core curriculum (e.g., English, social studies, science, and mathematics).

More often than not, it seems, quick writes are used to either spark student creativity in writing fictional and/or humorous stories or reflective pieces. What is often not appreciated by many teachers is that quick writes are also ideal for getting students to write about issues germane to the content of their English, social studies, science, or mathematics classes; and not only write, but to do so in ways that engage them, provoke them to think in creative ways and outside of the proverbial box, and to reflect on what they are about to learn, are learning or have learned.

We, the editors, firmly believe sound writing tasks generally support a high level of learning in all core subjects, and thus assist teachers to engage their students in inquiry, analysis, synthesis and evaluative activities.

THE VALUE OF QUICK WRITES

One of the greatest benefits of a quick write is that it provides the student with a quick, generally enjoyable, and painless way to "get" his/her ideas down. Another major benefit is that each quick write generally contains a kernel or spark (be it an idea, a phrase, a quirky take on a subject) that the student perceives as being worthy of extending and polishing later. Put another way, sometimes the writing generated in response to a quick write cries out to be crafted further through revision and publishing. Once in a while—if the timing, the focus of the quick write, the author's mood, and the muse are all just right—a piece may, like Athena, spring out of the writer's head fully formed. And at these moments, the activity is an end in itself.

Because quick writes are not used for grading or evaluation purposes, students feel a sense of freedom and safety in expression. Such "low stakes" writing assignments, according to Peter Elbow (1997), are essential for developing writing fluency: "If we assign lots of low stakes writing, students are much less liable to be held back by fear or inability to put what they know on paper when they come to high stakes writing" (p. 6). Furthermore, optional sharing after the writing time allows students the opportunity to share their drafts and receive feedback in the form of applause or positive comments. This, too, promotes the goal of a supportive writing community in the classroom.

Unfortunately, there is ample evidence that many teachers still do not teach their students the value of prewriting. Research, though, clearly shows that prewriting is an essential skill to successful writing. *Writing Next* (Graham & Perin, 2007) includes prewriting as 1 of 11 strategies that research indicates are most effective for improving the writing of students in Grades 4-12. Graves and Piche (1989) noted that research shows that even having students "list their own words for a topic before writing about it produces longer and qualitatively better texts" (p. 15). They also assert that research shows that "students involved in a variety of peer group prewriting topic discussions produce more extensive writing" (Graves & Piche, 1989, p. 15). They go on to say that "other [useful] activities include listing key ideas associated with topics and constructing idea charts or trees which depict relationships between ideas. The application of these prewriting activities would be equally effective for writing undertaken in science, social studies, history, and so on" (Graves & Piche, 1989, p. 15).

It is critical for teachers to be conversant with this research, and it is even more critical for them to act on it. More specifically, teachers at all levels and in all subjects need to teach students both the value of prewriting (e.g., to generate ideas and to make connections between various thoughts before attempting to construct a piece of writing) and techniques for making regular use of prewriting activities. Teaching such strategies is neither time-consuming nor difficult, and the dividends in regard to the quantity and quality of what students write are enormous.

Underscoring the critical need to have students engage in prewriting activities prior to the act of composing, Kingen (1994) argues, quite convincingly, that teachers must teach students "how to engage in various activities more effectively, especially prewriting and revising. [Furthermore,] students should have opportunities to experience concrete activities in the classroom which build their information base(s)" (p. 98). That is precisely what a quick write can accomplish.

Prewriting for prewriting's sake, though, is often counterproductive. For example, in some classrooms students are only taught one, two or, at the most, three prewriting strategies; and then, gravitating to one over the others, they often end up using the same method over and over again (e.g., brainstorming, clustering, outlining, free-writing) to the point where the process either becomes boring, mechanical, or both for the student. The end result is that the use of prewriting is less powerful and effective than it could or should be. In *Best Practices in Writing Instruction*, Newell, Koukis, and Boster (2007) make the following argument for meaningful writing tasks: "To function successfully, writing activities must be structured to support and value the role of exploration and discovery" (p. 78). Well developed quick writes are generally creative and/or thought-provoking tasks that are capable of igniting student thought, passion, and the flow of writing. But since each quick write is unique, *not formulaic*, and can and should cover a broad gamut of topics, issues, and interests—all developed for the express purpose of sparking instant interest in potential writers— one rarely finds students bored with quick writes.

QUICK WRITES AND STUDENT PORTFOLIOS

Each quick write can result in a new rough draft, and as a result each student accumulates a body of varied drafts. Within designated parameters, students need to be allowed some freedom to choose the pieces on which they want to continue working. As these drafts are added to students' writing portfolios, their choices from which to draw increases.

This is important, for students generally do their best work when they care about the piece on which they are working. This holds true in any subject on any project, but is especially true with writing.

The frequent use of quick writes also contributes to the National Writing Project's assertion that "schools not only need to have students write more; they must also give students a rich and diverse array of writing experiences" (National Writing Project & Nagin, 2003, p. 15).

USING QUICK WRITES IN THE CLASSROOM

Herein, one of the coeditors, Shelley Dirst, a former high school English teacher who is now with the Arkansas Department of Education, delineates why and how she used quick writes in her classroom:

In my high school English classes, I used the quick write concept to accomplish several goals. First, I wanted to help students learn to get words on paper faster, with less effort, minimizing the agony of writer's block. I knew they would need this skill when faced with performance assessments such as the state's literacy assessments or classroom essay tests in any subject. So, quick writes were practice exercises to help my students learn to write with confidence under time constraints no matter the topic or question.

Second, I wanted them to build a store of writing ideas, story starters, and first drafts to fill their writers' notebooks. This way, when we conducted a more independent writer's workshop approach (one that would be more student-directed rather than teacher-assigned), they would be armed with ideas for individual pieces that they could take through the writing process. This would help alleviate the dreaded, "I have nothing to write about!" complaints that often elicited the banal responses typical of compulsory assignments. Moreover, the mere notion that writing could be abandoned, stored for a future use, or worked into another draft would raise students' awareness of and immersion in the concept of process writing.

Third, I wanted to create a climate of excitement about writing, one that could replace the high-pressure, error-focused world of classroom writing that seems to build in intensity as high-stakes performance assessments pervade our classrooms. Part of creating this enjoyment and personal engagement with writing would be to emphasize student choice, empowering the writer rather than forcing all kids to write the essay on, for example, "Which American would you most like to meet?" (5 pages typed, final draft due Friday). Instead, we would have fun, be silly, start things we would never finish, write things just for the sheer joy of writing and for sharing aloud if we wanted. We would show off, cut up, and listen to each other, teacher included.

Fourth, I wanted to write with the students. I would model for them, imperfections and all. I would put us all on the same footing as writers who have something to say and who deserve to be heard.

So, this is what I did. First, I slowly introduced them to quick writes. I led a few based on children's books, popular songs, paintings, newspaper articles, and pieces of literature from our textbooks. In the beginning, I had to prod some reluctant students to write without editing themselves, to just say whatever came out of their pens (as Peter Elbow would suggest). I found that writing was difficult for many students at first; some had written only one line at the end of five minutes. Slowly, however, they warmed up to the idea, saw that it was not risky, and gained the skill of filling the page. With practice, they became more fluent, gaining confidence and letting go a little.

The next term, I threw them a curve. Each student was assigned to develop and lead a quick write for his/her class. Each selected a Friday on which to conduct it, and thus every Friday became "Quick Write Day." On Fridays, the class was totally directed by the students presenting their quick writes. On Fridays, I sat in a student desk rather than standing up front or moving throughout the room. On Fridays, we all wrote and shared and laughed and even cried. Certainly, some student-created quick writes elicited stronger responses than others. But the best part was that because the assignments were created and conducted by their peers, they were even more meaningful to the students than the ones I had created. Everyone anticipated Friday's class, and everyone was engaged.

As students began to assemble their writing portfolios, I challenged them to return to their quick write folders and create new pieces of writing from the raw material they found there. Our work on this project led us to hone revision skills and to examine the power of experimenting with different genres to best express an idea.

Without realizing it, the students were learning. Learning to write on demand, learning to develop their writing voice, learning from each other about how many forms, approaches, styles, etc. can emerge from one, if you will, "prompt" (a sense that there is more than one right way to approach a piece of writing). Before they realized what was happening, they were having fun. And what's more, many of them gained a sense of their potential. They surprised themselves when they wrote something powerful that made people think, laugh, or cry, and they realized that they do have something to say. In this way, we had created a classroom of writers.

CONCLUSION

Each of the quick writes presented in this book follows the same non-threatening format. The quick writes have been designed to motivate writers to write quickly from the head *and/or* the heart. The latter is a combination that often results in unique, honest and powerful ideas, insights, stories, and vignettes waiting to be expressed. We believe that quick writes constitute one of the most powerful prewriting strategies currently in practice.

Writers engaged in quick write activities begin to explore their thoughts, insights, ideas, themselves, others, and the world around them. They also begin to develop a genuine enjoyment of writing, and through sharing, a writing community can flourish. Once this shift occurs, the possibilities are endless.

We hope that this book will inspire each student to discover the writer within. We believe that both you and your students will be amazed at the stories they already have inside themselves that are just waiting to be accessed. So, we welcome you to join us in sparking the brain and igniting the pen!

REFERENCES

Elbow, P. (1997, Spring). High stakes and low stakes in assigning and responding to writing. Writing to Learn: Strategies for Assigning and Responding to Writing Across the Disciplines. *New Directions for Teaching and Learning, 69*, 5-13.

Graham, S., & Perin, D. (2007). *Writing next: Effective strategies to improve writing of adolescents in middle and high schools—A report to Carnegie Corporation of New York*. Washington, DC: Alliance for Excellent Education.

Graves, M., & Piche, G. (1989). Knowledge about reading and writing. In M. C. Reynolds (Ed.), *Knowledge base for the beginning teacher* (pp. 207-219). New York: Pergamon Press.

Kingen, S. (1994). When middle school students compose: An examination of processes and products. *Research in Middle Level Education, 18*(1): 83-103.

National Writing Project & Nagin, C. (2003). *Because writing matters: Improving student writing in our schools*. San Francisco: Jossey-Bass.

Newell, G. E., Koukis, S., & Boster, S. (2007). Best practices in developing a writing across the curriculum program in secondary school. In S. Graham, C. A. MacArthur, & J. Fitzgerald (Eds.), *Best practices in writing instruction* (pp. 74-98). New York: The Guilford Press.

ENGLISH LANGUAGE ARTS

IMAGINATION

Got Warts?

Sharla Keen-Mills
8th-Grade English Teacher,
Woodland Junior High School, Fayetteville, Arkansas

Directions:

The teacher should read the excerpt from *The Adventures of Tom Sawyer* below.

In *The Adventures of Tom Sawyer*, Mark Twain creates a conversation between Huck Finn and Tom Sawyer regarding the removal of warts. On his way to school, Tom comes upon the "juvenile pariah of the village, Huckleberry Finn," carrying a dead cat, and he asks, "Say, what is dead cats good for, Huck?"

"Good for? Cure warts with," Huck replies. Then Tom tries to convince Huck that "spunk-water" is better, but his curiosity about the use of dead cats to cure warts prompts him to ask Huck about the procedure.

Huck replies that you stand by the grave of an evil person "long about midnight," wait for the devil to come along to take "that feller away," and then, "you heave your cat after 'em and say, 'Devil follow corpse, cat fol-

Spark the Brain, Ignite the Pen: Quick Writes for Kindergarten Through High School Teachers and Beyond, 2nd Edition, pp. 3–11

3

low devil, warts follow cat, I'm done with ye!' That'll fetch any wart," Huck tells Tom.

Make sure students know what a pariah is: pariah—pa-ri-ah—an outcast. A person who is rejected from society or home.

Ask: *What is your cure for warts? Take a few minutes and brainstorm some ideas:*

Where do you need to go to be cured of warts?
What time of the day or night would you need to go?
Who or what should you bring with you?
What other materials or tools should you take?
What would you do once you arrived at the appropriate location?
Is there a chant, song, or spell you would need to say?
Anything else?

Write for 5–10 minutes explaining your wart cure.
Share as time allows.

Reflection:

I use this quick write when I am teaching exposition. Students practice organizing their information, writing specific topic sentences and using specific supporting evidence (reasons, details, facts, and commentary) to support their topic. Some students have also turned this quick write into poetry and "news" articles.

REFERENCE

Twain, M. (1980). *The adventures of Tom Sawyer.* New York: Scholastic.

You Picked a Fine Time to Leave Me Lucille

Sharla Keen-Mills
8th-Grade English Teacher,
Woodland Junior High School, Faytteville, Arkansas

Directions:

Ask students if they believe in ghosts. Ask if they know of any haunted houses. If anyone does, ask him or her to share a personal ghost or haunted house story with the other students.

Next, read the newspaper story (see the appendix to this piece) about a haunted house in Fayetteville, Arkansas, or any other story about haunted houses or missing persons.

Share with the students that Lucille really did disappear. She was a young wife who went out the door to fix her husband's breakfast, and was never seen again—or so he said. Spend the next few minutes writing an explanation of what happened to Lucille—or write about your own personal haunting experience.

Allow students to share their writing.

Reflection:

Our school is located very close to the house where Mrs. Johnson disappeared, so my students and I discuss the proximity of the railroad tracks to the house, the extent of the woods and fields surrounding the house, what might have been going on in our town in the 1920s, and any other "evidence" before we write about Mrs. Johnson. Again, any story of a disappearance anywhere could be used for this exercise. In fact, I've done this activity without even telling the students about the hauntings. Instead, I just tell them where Lucille lived and explain the circumstances of her disappearance. Having a local story is meaningful to my students, and they have come up with everything from their own parodies, to limericks, feature news articles, and grisly scripts for television series such as *C.S.I.*, *Without a Trace*, and *Cold Case* explaining what happened to her. I have never failed to have several students turn this quick write into a polished piece.

REFERENCE

Garrett, R. (1996, October 30). Old restaurant still has plenty of spirit. *Northwest Arkansas Times*, pp. C1, C3.

APPENDIX

"Old Restaurant Still Has Plenty of Spirit"

By Rusty Garrett
Times Staff Writer

The ghost at the now-closed Farmer's Daughter Restaurant seems to be doing very little haunting these days. But Doris McClelland, owner of the house that once operated as a popular Fayetteville restaurant, is convinced the spirits watch over her and the 30-acre wooded site off North Gregg Avenue.

McClelland believes the ghost in the turn-of-the-century house is that of Lucille Johnson, a young woman who vanished from the property one day in 1926.

Johnson, a cousin of the Nettleship family who owned the dairy farm and house, moved there in the 1920s to attend the University of Arkansas. She eventually married and stayed on in a small dwelling on the property.

According to legend, Johnson did all her cooking in the nearby main house, and left her shack one morning to prepare breakfast for her husband. She disappeared and was never seen again. McClelland learned of Johnson shortly after she and her husband bought the site in 1972 with the idea of enlarging the house and opening a restaurant. An elderly man, who went by the name Morning Glory, had worked at the dairy farm where the house is located at the time Johnson disappeared. He was overseeing some of the restoration work.

McClelland said Morning Glory had balked at her request to retrieve a weathered brass bed from a weed-covered lot on the property. The man told her, "Mrs. Johnson wouldn't want the bed disturbed, because it had been in her house when she left the farm." Morning Glory told McClelland the story of Johnson. She learned even more about her disappearance from several area restaurateurs who also helped her assemble a menu for her restaurant and club.

McClelland met Johnson shortly after that. She was staying alone in the house while her husband settled family affairs in Houston. The house was outfitted with a security system, but police advised her to leave an upstairs light on and lock her bedroom door before retiring each night. One night she failed to do either. She said she awoke at 3:00 AM to the sound of a car barreling down the private drive. "I got up and started toward the door to get it shut," she said. "Before I got there the door shut and locked. Then the light in the hall came on." The police, responding to the silent alarm, arrived at the house 10 minutes later and made a fruitless search for intruders.

McClelland said although she is easily frightened, the incident did not shake her. She said as she entered a small upstairs room, she sensed a "presence" on the other side of the door. She likened it to the feeling someone is watching you as you sleep.

"It was the most comfortable, safe feeling I believe I've ever had in my life," she said. She said she knew it was the spirit of Johnson, "and she's never left me." While Johnson has offered McClelland a measure of comfort, she also has proven a tireless—and tiresome prankster.

"She's not having much fun now. But when we had the restaurant, she had a ball. But you never saw her," McClelland said. Johnson would regularly close windows in the kitchen, even when they were propped open with stout 2-by-4' braces. She delighted in moving items around on tables that had been set up for customers. McClelland said the ghost enjoyed rearranging figurines and knick-knacks on shelves attached to the windows of a glass patio over-looking the restaurant grounds. In reaction to that, McClelland glued the items to the shelves. It solved the problem, but McClelland laments that the shelves will have to be broken if she ever wants to move the figurines.

Johnson was wildly unpopular with the restaurant workers, many of them university students who were allowed to come in a bit later on a Sunday morning if they took the time to clean up and prepare tables after closing Saturday night. Johnson would gleefully attack the carefully set tables over-night, undoing the employees' work. "Everybody saw it done, and the kids didn't like it," McClelland said.

On one morning of a hectic Razorback football game weekend, "after she had been really bad," McClelland said, Johnson apparently felt it necessary to present her a peace offering. Upon a piano in the restaurant, she found an ancient iron mirror, an item "old enough that Mrs. Johnson could have had it in her house." She said there was no other explanation for how it came to be in the restaurant on the piano. She keeps the mirror in a bathroom and says some of her guests are afraid to enter the room after they have heard the story. "It never gave me any trouble," McClelland said of the mirror. "But I don't ever look in it. I don't even dust it."

"We never, ever got over Mrs. Johnson being a problem," when operating the restaurant, Mrs. McClelland said. But it was ultimately her husband's health problems that led them to close The Farmer's Daughter in 1984. Johnson is very much a member of the McClelland family. When the dozen members of the family gather at the house for the holidays, she is much dis-cussed and sometimes makes "her presence known."

McClelland said her son, Kirk, and his wife each year witness a mysterious light that travels around an upstairs dining room. "There is not a single per-son in this family... who laughs at the legend," McClelland said.

That is not to say that Johnson doesn't have a sense of humor. The McClel-lands each year put on a family show that family members take turns writing. Three years ago, the title of the program was "Whatever Happened to Mrs. Johnson?" The show was a 2-$\frac{1}{2}$-hour spoof of the Johnson legend.

McClelland said it was about 10:00 PM on a snowy night when her son, who was videotaping the production, led family members outside for the final shot. As he began to tape the scene, he was distracted and aimed the camera at the top floor of the house. When the family viewed the tape later, they saw through the windows a figure carrying a light, walking the length of the upper room. "It's the only time any of us have ever seen her," McClelland said. "She was so tickled by a 2-$\frac{1}{2}$-hour show about Mrs. Johnson that she decided to walk across." Otherwise, Johnson has been pretty quiet in recent years.

"I don't ever get any visions of her, or any noise from her or hear steps from her," McClelland said. However, last Halloween, KFSM-TV did a story on Johnson as part of a week-long series on ghosts. The film crew was headed upstairs to film the attic room where the woman stayed when she lived in the house and the door inexplicably slammed shut and would not open. "She's a very private woman," McClelland said. "When the camera man hit the top of the stairs, the door shut. They pushed and pulled. They could never get it open. It scared them to death." Eventually a carpenter was called, who had to cut the door from its frame to open the room.

McClelland is as protective of Johnson as the ghost is of her. She said she once had an offer from a Wal-Mart executive to buy the house. He had heard there was a ghost on the premises, and he said he himself had a ghost that had traveled with him to Arkansas. McClelland said she told the man the house was not for sale. An alternate offer was made to rent the house for a seance. McClelland refused. "I think Mrs. Johnson would have been horrified to be put on the level where they rock tables," she said.

Wanted: An Heir for a $375,000 Estate

Samuel Totten
Director of the Northwest Arkansas Writing Project,
University of Arkansas, Fayetteville

Directions:
Over the years, I've found that newspaper articles about quirky subjects are outstanding sources for quick write ideas. I came across this idea—an old man looking for a suitable heir—in the *Northwest Arkansas Times*. It was a personal-interest story that served as "filler" in between more newsworthy pieces.

I simply read the story to the students, and then have them respond in letter format.

Wanted: An Heir for a $375,000 Estate

By Steve Karnowski

Minneapolis: Clayton Goward has a $375,000 estate but no suitable heir. His solution? An add in the *Star Tribune* newspaper.

"My estate is sizable and I have no worthy heirs," the July 11 ad said. "I need a solution now. If you have an answer, please write."

As of Thursday, the 79-year old Goward had received 32 responses. Some of the letters came from people who told him they were in dire straits and could use his money. Some were from churches and charities. Others just contained advice, such as the note from a sheriff who "had nothing to say but be careful," Goward said.

Goward is not sure what he's looking for, but he knows none of the letters has particularly moved him. "I hope I haven't opened up a can of worms," he said.

Goward got divorced long ago, and his three sons grew up with their mother in northern Minnesota. He lived in Minneapolis then and didn't see them much. Their relationships are still strained, though he said he has tried to make amends, visiting them occasionally and giving them money. "When they were young, I wasn't with them. I can understand that. But I'm a better person now," he said.

Goward had colon cancer surgery in December, and although he is recovering very well, he has no way of knowing how much longer he will live. He said his house and his 13 acre lot about 60 miles north of Minneapolis, plus his other investments, easily bring his net worth up to $375,000. "I would like to be able to leave it to someone who loves me, but I haven't found anybody like that," he said. Clayton Goward's address is Rt. 1, Box 248C, Pine City, Minn. 55063.

Reflection:
Many of the students, as they say, "really get into it," for they are keen on actually coming up with an idea as to how they can convince the old man that they have *the solution*! Others treat the subject tongue in cheek and have fun with it. In fact, most pieces the students write in response to this activity are quite humorous.

REFERENCE

Karnowski, S. (1999, August 4). *Northwest Arkansas Times*, p. A4.

"Bearly" Work

Martha Pierce
3rd-Grade Teacher,
T.G. Smith Elementary School, Springdale, Arkansas

Directions:
Tell the students that you are going to read a favorite story of yours, and one that they have probably heard many times. Read the story *Goldilocks and the Three Bears*. Tell the students that it is now one year after the end of the story. Ask a few questions to get the students thinking, such as: *What have the three bears been doing this past year? How might their lives have*

changed in the past year? What might have caused the changes? Do they still live in the forest? If not, where do they live? Do they still have porridge for breakfast? If not, why? What might they have instead?

Next, show the students the three bears brought to class for this purpose. Tell them they have 5 minutes to write down what they think has happened to the three bears. Call time after 5 minutes and allow students to share theirs with the class.

Reflection:

The kids love this activity! They love the creativity it involves, and can hardly wait to share their stories. What more could we ask for?

Materials:

Three stuffed bears of varying sizes.

REFERENCE

Any copy of *Goldilocks and the Three Bears*.

A Picture Paints a Thousand Words

Clare Lesieur
4th-Grade Teacher,
Skyline Heights Elementary School, Harrison, Arkansas

and

Mary Wince
Coordinator of Gifted Education,
Valley Springs School, Valley Springs, Arkansas

Directions:

Prior to conducting this quick write, you will need to collect at least as many photographs as there are students in your class. The more photographs your students have to choose from, the better. We accumulated a good collection of old black-and-white photos from antique stores and flea markets.

Read the "Acknowledgments" page from Lois Lowry's (2002) *The Silent Boy:*

Few things give me more pleasure than looking at photographs. To glimpse other lives, caught and captured in moments that live on long after the circumstances of the moment have passed, makes me shiver with imagination. All of the people in these photographs are real people. Some of them were people I knew and loved. One is my own mother. Others are strangers. But people who knew them generously allowed me to use them to illustrate this story.

In particular, I want to thank Betty Landis Carson, who sent me some photos from her own family collection; and Rex and Phyllis Naylor, who did as well. But there is no way to thank the people whose family photographs ended up in the New Hampshire antique store where I found them. I find myself wondering about those beautiful children, those wide-eyed young girls, those sturdy young men—all of them captured by a camera in the early part of the [20th] century when cameras were still a novelty. Someone must have treasured their pictures once. Someone knew their names and what their stories were. Now I have turned them into fiction. I can only hope they wouldn't mind. (n.p.)

Next, show the examples of old photographs from Lois Lowry's book. Then, display the collection of photographs you have available for your students to use as prompts for their writing. Students should look through the pictures and select ones that spark story ideas. Students may make a connection to their own lives or create a completely fictional account based on the photos. Allow time to share and show photographs when finished.

Reflection:

We conducted this quick write with a group of teachers and were pleasantly surprised by the powerful writing that ensued. We did have some difficulty finding old photographs at a reasonable price. One suggestion would be to scan family photos and use the copies with your students.

REFERENCE

Lowry, L. (2003). *The silent boy.* New York: Houghton Mifflin.

LISTS

What I Know/Don't Know:
In Search of Research Topics

Denise Nemec
Composition Teacher,
Northwest Arkansas Community College, Bentonville, Arkansas

Directions:

I ask the students to get out any previous writings that share their experiences and interests. I explain that they will use those writings as a base for the upcoming writing activity. I then share my own list of what I know/don't know:

1. I know how to play basketball, softball, and volleyball, but I do not know how to coach those sports.
2. I know how to clean a house and mow a yard, but I do not know how to build a house or plan a landscape or garden.
3. I know I am appalled by the genocide happening in the Darfur region of the Sudan, but I do not know what I can do to help stop it.

Spark the Brain, Ignite the Pen: Quick Writes for Kindergarten Through High School Teachers and Beyond, 2nd Edition, pp. 13–33

4. I know I want to travel in Europe for several months, but I do not know how to do this affordably and safely.

5. I know I want to attend a writing retreat, but I do not know where these take place, how much they cost, or how to get into one.

6. I know I want to use my car less, but I do not know what my options are for alternative transportation or how to make car pooling work.

7. I know I am concerned about global warming, but I do not know all of the things I can do on a personal level to help stop it or slow it down.

I then give them about 10–15 minutes to come up with their own statements.

Samples from Student Lists:

1. I know I want to get a job with the [Arkansas] Game and Fish Commission, but I don't know what degree they would most likely want from an applicant. —Chris

2. I know I want to be more outgoing, but I don't know how to start. —Whitney

3. I do know how to play the piano and read notation. I don't know how to intuitively express myself and [my] emotions musically. — Martin

4. I do know that Fidel Castro is ill and will probably die soon. I don't know what that means for the Cuban socialist regime or Cuban citizens. ——Martin

5. I know how to shop, but I don't know how to save money. —Amy

6. I know how to get a job. I don't know how to keep it. —Kyle

7. I know what a great film is and how to create some aspects, but I don't know the best way to start [making my own film]. —Grant

8. I know most of what people do is trivial. I don't know why we let the trivial govern our lives. —Josh

Reflection:

This quick write activity is a variation of Sam Totten's "What I Know," published in the first edition of *Spark the Brain, Ignite the Pen*. I teach freshman composition in a community college, and since my classes do not meet every day, it is often necessary to milk the most out of the few precious minutes we have. This writing activity helps my students appreciate how what we know may be the place to start in understanding what we do not know.

My students seemed to enjoy looking at things from this unusual angle. It opened their eyes to the learning possibilities that are around us all the time, and in some cases, it leads them to seek knowledge when they might not have otherwise. At the very least, it aroused a stronger sense of self-awareness and allowed them to see themselves a little more clearly.

The above-quoted students were in my spring 2007, Comp I class, and they have given their permission for me to use their words here. The ideas expressed in the first two examples became those students' topics for their research papers. In the case of Martin, he has decided recently to major in piano performance. I know he wanted to better express himself emotionally when playing the piano, but I do not know if his efforts to do so are what inspired him to declare musical performance-piano for his major. I guess I'll have to do a little research to find out.

Are You More Like?

Jackie Hassel
9th-Grade English Teacher,
Ramay Junior High School, Fayetteville, Arkansas

Directions:

I inform my students of the following: *I'm going to provide you, orally, with pairs of words. As I give you the pair, I want you to jot down both words and then circle one of the two that you are more like. For example, if I give you the two words "cold" and "warm," you would simply write both words down on the same line and then circle the one that best describes you.*

Initially, some of the choices may seem odd, so you have to play along. In certain cases you may even think, "Neither choice describes me." In such a situation you need to pick the one that you are most comfortable with. In the end you will see that it all makes sense.

OK, here we go:

ARE YOU MORE LIKE
breakfast or dinner?
summer or winter?
the country or the city?
the present or the future?

the tortoise or the hare?
a VW bug or a Corvette?
patent leather or suede?
a paddle or a ping-pong ball?
a computer or a ballpoint pen?
a rock band or a string quartet?
a fly swatter or fly paper?
a mountain or a valley?
"a stitch in time" or "better late than never"?
a screened porch or a picture window?
a babbling brook or a placid lake?
Niagara Falls or Mount St. Helens?
a motorcycle or a tricycle?
a roller skate or a pogo stick?
yellow or blue?
fire or water?
earth or air?
grasshopper or ant?
spring or fall?

OK, now choose one comparison and explain, in detail, how you are like the word that you chose.

Reflection:

I find that 5–10 options at a time work best with my students. I also give my students the option to generate other pairs of words if they wish to do so. Students generally love this activity as the results are, in various cases, humorous, serious, sassy, and reflective.

Promises, Promises, Promises

Helen Eaton
4th-Grade Teacher,
Holcomb Elementary School, Fayetteville, Arkansas

Directions:

Think about the synonyms of "promise." Although they mean the same thing, each carries its own connotation. Promise, vow, resolution, pact, your word, covenant, pledge, and so on. Think about the many types and levels of promises. Whether broken or kept, promises can be life changing or their importance may fade with time as they are forgotten. I'm going to share a collection of objects, pictures, books, and thoughts that represent promises from my own life. As I do so, think about the promises that you have made, those that you have kept and those that you have broken. Now take a minute or two and jot them down. You don't need full sentences; notes are fine. Think about promises that have been made to you, those that have been kept and those that have been broken. Take a minute and jot these down. Now, write about a promise, vow, commitment, or resolution that has had an impact on your life.

Examples of promises:

New Year's resolutions—lose 10 pounds, eat more healthily, slow down, exercise.

Brownie Beenie—Girl Scout pledge to be a good citizen and always leave a place cleaner than you found it.

BFFE Charm—Best Friends Forever charm necklace from Debby, my very best friend in school. We gave our word to always be close. We have lost touch over the years.

High School Annual—All the signatures and secret pacts on those last pages. "We'll always keep in touch. Our kids will grow up to be friends," Tamra. Who was Tamra anyway?

Cake Bride and Groom—My husband and I took the marriage vows 16 years ago. That love continues to grow with each year.

Baby's Hospital Cap—Many promises were whispered to my newborns as I spent the first nights in the hospital with them. No commitment or bond is as strong as between a mother and child. It's not always easy. I will always love them.

American Flag—We begin every morning, "I pledge allegiance to the flag of the United States of America." How often do I really listen to those words?

Contract—I am legally bound to come to work and do my job. It doesn't mention all the extra hours.

50th Anniversary Picture—My parents' celebration of 50 years together shows true commitment. They are an inspiration.

Examples of promises in literature:

Charlotte's Web—Charlotte promises to save Wilbur's life. She writes words on her web to save him.

Where the Red Fern Grows—Billy makes a vow to himself to get hunting dogs. He works to earn the money. On their first hunting trip, he promises the dogs that if they'll tree a coon, he'll do the rest. They tree a coon in the biggest tree. Keeping the promise turns out to be much harder than expected.

Dear Mr. Henshaw—Leigh loses faith in his father after he continually fails to keep his promises to call or to send his child support.

"Stopping by Woods on a Snowy Evening" by Robert Frost:

The woods are lovely, dark, and deep,
But I have promises to keep,
And miles to go before I sleep,
And miles to go before I sleep.

Reflection:

This quick write was created for a beginning-of-the-year Northwest Arkansas Writing Project quarterly meeting. The fact that many of us make promises to ourselves and to others at the beginning of new years prompted the idea to look closely at that tradition and at promises in general. This quick write was done with a group of adults who consider themselves writers, but I believe it is a topic that could be adapted for children of any age quite easily by choosing symbols of promises to which they could relate. There was actually very little group sharing after this piece of writing was completed. After the meeting, several shared that it had prompted some very personal writing. As I reflect on the nature of the topic, that should not surprise me. Promises, whether kept or broken, are often very personal. I believe that some powerful writing can come from this quick write.

REFERENCES

Cleary, B. (1994). *Dear Mr. Henshaw*. New York: Avon Camelot.

Frost, R. (1978). *Stopping by woods on a snowy evening*. New York: E. P. Dutton.

Rawls, W. (1961). *Where the red fern grows*. New York: Bantam Books.

White, E. B. (1952). *Charlotte's web*. New York: HarperTrophy.

100 Things To Do Before You Die!

Anne Lane
9th-Grade English Teacher,
Ramay Junior High School, Fayetteville, Arkansas

Directions:

Here's how I introduce and use this activity with my ninth graders:

The Tulsa World *conducted a survey of more than 350 people responding to the question, "What should people do and experience before they die?" Readers ages 6–90 contributed to the list of "100 Things To Do Before You Die."*

Here are some of the suggestions offered by the readers:

Be instrumental in changing a law.
See Mark McGwire hit a home run.
Put your hand in wet concrete.
Ride a bike as fast as you can down a ramp into a lake.
Look up at the giant redwoods.
Have an invention marketed and patented.
Visit all 50 states.
Sky dive.
Visit the country your ancestors call home.
Play in the snow.
Write a book about your life.
Fall in love, get your heart broken, and fall in love again.
Dance in the rain.
Ditch school at least once.
Give a speech in front of a large crowd.
Read "Walden" by Henry David Thoreau, Catcher in the Rye *by J.D. Salinger, and* The Scarlet Ibis *by James Hurst.*
Learn to play an instrument.
Run a marathon.
Learn a foreign language.
Play peek-a-boo with a 2-year-old.
Live abroad for a year in a small village in England.
See America from a motorcycle.

I thought about what I would put on my list of things I want to do before I die, and I came up with the following:

Snorkel in the ocean.
Have a book published.
Visit Ireland (just because); visit Holland where my maternal grandfather's
    parents immigrated from.
Live on a beach and walk on it early in the morning alone.
See my children fall in love and get married.
Have a grandchild.
See my children financially independent.
Visit the rebuilt Globe in Stratford and see a Shakespearean play there.
Meet and visit with Carol Burnett, Patti Duke, Sally Field, Madeleine L'Engle,
    and Barbara Kingsolver.
Have my book featured on the Oprah Winfrey Show.
Stay in a chateau in Switzerland and ski.

A year ago, I had the opportunity to snorkel in the Caribbean when my sister took me on a vacation to Cancun. I even thought, "Oh wow, I get to check something off my list!" It was awesome. The turquoise water was as clear as a swimming pool. I felt like Jacques Cousteau. The reefs were beautiful and intricate—natural-made castles that aquariums can only dream about with brightly dressed exotic fish gliding in and out. Now I want to do it again!

Have you made such a list? What would you include and why? What experiences have you had already that would have gone on such a list?

Free-write for about 4–5 minutes compiling your list.

Now choose one wish or experience and expand on it. Write for 5–7 minutes.

I always have three to five students share.

Reflection:

I have not only shared this quick write with teachers in the Northwest Arkansas Writing Project, but it is a favorite of many of my ninth-grade students. These are a few of their wishes:

- Stop world hunger
- Adopt 10 kids
- Find a cure for cancer
- Get a tattoo
- Meet my real dad
- See my mom not in pain
- Live one day without worrying about what people think of me

- Find true love that lasts
- Go on a road/camping trip on Harley Davidsons with my friends
- Make a disabled kid's dream come true
- See a kangaroo
- Milk a cow
- Hang glide over the Grand Canyon
- Throw the biggest party ever

This quick write has worked successfully when I meet with a group for the first time. Everyone has something to say, and the writing can be impersonal and nonthreatening if the participants choose to share. It's always a lot of fun, but can also be the impetus for some great pieces.

REFERENCE

Collington, J. (2001, April 15). 100 things to do before you die. *Tulsa World*, p. D1.

What's It Like to Wait?

Jeanne King
*Gifted and Talented Teacher,
Holt Middle School, Fayetteville, Arkansas*

Directions:
We've all had to wait for things in our lives. Here's the story of how Madeleine L'Engle waited to have a publisher accept her manuscript for A Wrinkle in Time. *What I wish to have you do is read the short essay, "Anesthetics," from* Miracle on 10th Street *by Madeleine L'Engle.*

Once you've completed reading the essay, think of those times when you have had to wait for something. Quickly jot down a list of such times. Once you have listed 5–10 items, select one of them and write about that special time or something that you had to wait for, how it felt to wait, and if it was worth the wait. You have 5 minutes to write, and then those who wish to share shall have a chance to do so.

Reflection:
This quick write was used at a follow-up meeting to the Northwest Arkansas Writing Project's Invitational Summer Writing Institute. The fol-

low-up was held in December, when waiting and anticipation were in the air due to the holiday season. One woman in the group had just had a baby; "waiting" was particularly relevant to her. All of the writings were personal and provided insights into how humans handle waiting in different ways. This quick write would be ideal for all ages.

REFERENCE

L'Engle, M. (1998). *Miracle on 10th Street*. Wheaton, IL: Harold Shaw.

What Would You Do?

Denise (Nese) Nemec
Composition Instructor,
Northwest Arkansas Community College

Directions:
Several months ago, I bought blues musician Anthony Gomes's compact disc titled *Unity*. I was struck by the song "If You Could Rule the World," which has a strong message and thought-provoking question. His message is that the world is filled with crime, pollution, hate, segregation, guns, and lack of education, and his question is, "What would you do if you could rule the world?" Gomes indicates that some of the things we might try to do to change the world are not effective because freedom can be flighty, hard to ground, and idealism can burn too hot and fierce. He indicates that we must "fight a revolution" in order to "bring some resolution" to these problems, but that, ultimately, the only way we can truly change anything is to change ourselves first. That led me to consider what I would do if I could change things about myself that might lead to a change in the world.

My list:

- Conserve and protect the earth by walking more and using less water.
- Share more of my time and resources with those who need or could use them.
- Explain things more clearly so that people know what I am asking of them.

- Be a more active and involved citizen.
- Turn off the television.
- Learn to speak a second language.
- Show respect for everyone.
- Stop interrupting people when they are talking.

Free-write for 3–4 minutes to create a list of things you might change about yourself that could lead to a change in your world.

Mere days after discovering this song, I ran across another take on this idea in the cartoon strip called "Baby Blues." The oldest child, a daughter of about 5 years old, marches into the living room wearing a crown and cape. She proclaims that she is the boss of the world who gets anything she wants whenever she wants it. As her parents sit staring at her, she turns on her heel and announces that she is going to go think of a bunch of new things to want. In the last panel, her father remarks on her imagination, and her mother tells him that he's the one who has the imagination if he thinks his daughter is kidding.

What a fresh way of looking at things! Using this perspective, it was fun thinking of not-so-serious things I want for myself, things that might bring just as much positive change as the serious ideas.

I want:

- Belly laughs
- Rumpled clothes and no iron
- Time to play
- Time to talk
- Wild dancing
- A smile on everyone's face
- Everyone included
- Lots of sharing

Free-write for 3–4 minutes creating a list of fun and positive things you want in your life.

For my expanded writing, I chose the idea of sharing: When I share, I feel better about myself, my life, and the things that are happening around me. When I share, I seem to get back more than I have given. My sharing can be a generous smile or a commitment of time or money. Most often, I share honest compliments. Sharing positive, supportive thoughts changes my world because the people in my world become more positive and supportive. Maybe it's possible that this sort of sharing can change the world, can make us rulers of the worlds that we inhabit.

Have you ever thought of what you would do if you could change your world or yourself? What would you like to improve or change about your world or about who you are or the way you think or act? What might you take away? What might you add? How or why might your world or the world around you change?

Choose one aspect or item from your lists and expand on it. Write for 5–7 minutes. Have three to five participants share.

Reflection:

My childhood was somewhat strained due to my parents' divorce at a time (mid- to late 1960s) when few people did that and to the subsequent lower standard of living we fell to. Because time, funds, transportation, and options were limited, I often felt that I had no power or say in things that mattered. This created a feeling of disengagement from my world because I felt I had little power or control over it. Not surprisingly, I had little investment in it, either.

Fortunately, I did find my way out of such backward thinking. My journey toward self-discovery (which continues) seems to resonate with my students, who find it fascinating to learn about their teachers' inward lives. When students see that we continue to learn, seek to improve ourselves, and hope to make the world a better place in whatever big or small ways we can, then they (the students) are encouraged to do so, too. At the very least, my students seem to take away from this exercise the idea that who they are can make a difference, if they so choose.

I first tried "What Would You Do?" with my Freshman Composition II students at the community college where I teach. I shared the cartoon first and then the Gomes song. Although my students were able to create lists and then expand on one thing they would like to change, I felt that the order was wrong. I feel that the reversed order, song then cartoon, is more effective. Other songs, other cartoons, or other visuals could be used in this exercise. These two were what "came," literally, to me. Other songs or visuals that help us think about things a little differently would work just as well.

When I do this quick write, I do not read all that I have written about each of the two pieces. That saves some time, and it allows students to experience the pieces for themselves. I display the song's lyrics on an overhead projector while the song is playing, and then I reveal the cartoon panel by panel (four small ones as in the daily paper, not the large Sunday comics).

I usually write with my students. When it comes time to share and if no one volunteers, I break the ice and read my expanded piece. Usually, after that, several people want to share. In the ideal situation, we can segue from the exercise to one or more of the pieces of literature we read, study, and write about in the course. Perhaps a character demonstrates the same trait that a student wants to add to or take away from herself. Perhaps the plot of a story or play is similar to some part of a student's life or the life the student hopes for. When my students make these connections between the literature and their own lives, they and their essays light up.

REFERENCES

Gomes, A. (2002). If you could rule the world. In *Unity* [CD]. Anthony Gomes Music.

Kirkman, R., & Scott, J. (2004). *Baby blues*. King Features Syndicate.

Who Is an Expert?

Rebecca Cantey
10th-Grade English Teacher,
Bentonville High School, Bentonville, Arkansas

Directions:

The way in which I introduce this quick write to my high school students is as follows:

I was looking at all the magazines that seem to collect at my house, and it made me think about all the experts who write for magazines. There are experts to tell you:

- *What to eat* (hold up a food magazine like *Cooking Light, Southern Living,* or *Weight Watchers*)
- *What to watch, read, and listen to* (hold up an entertainment magazine like *Entertainment Weekly* or *TV Guide*)
- *Who is going to win* (hold up a sports magazine like *Sports Illustrated* or *ESPN the Magazine*)
- *How to raise children* (hold up a magazine like *Parents* or *American Baby*)
- *What to plant* (hold up a copy of *Better Homes and Gardens*)
- *What to wear* (hold up a copy of a fashion magazine like *Seventeen* or *Vogue*)
- *And then there is the famous expert who even tells us how to live* (hold up a copy of *Martha Stewart Living*).

This prompted me to begin thinking about all of the experts out in the world, as well as what it means to be an "expert." What do you think being an expert means? (Give 1–2 minutes for oral responses.) *The dictionary says that expert means "A person having great knowledge, experience, or skill in a certain field." I thought about this, and I made a list:*

I think I am an expert at:

- *Making chocolate chip cookies*
- *Singing*
- *Watching football*
- *Scrapbooking*
- *Shooting a basketball*
- *Writing*
- *Playing Guesstures*
- *American literature*

If you look at the list you will notice that some things require talent (singing), some require an interest or education (American literature), and some require experience (making chocolate chip cookies or shooting a basketball). Also notice that some things on my list are general (writing) and some are specific (shooting a basketball—not playing basketball generally because I'm slow and I can't jump). But my list is not complete, and thus I made another list:

I wish I were an expert at the following:

- *Tennis*
- *Snow skiing*
- *Mountain climbing*
- *Cleaning the house*
- *Sewing*

Now I want you to free write a list of what you think you are an expert at and then what you wish you were. You have 2 minutes.

Finally, I also came to the realization that all of these experts write about their expertise. They write about cooking, movies, sports, gardening, child psychology, fashion, and living. Now I want you to take one of your examples of your expertise or examples of what you wish you had expertise in and expand on it. Write for 5–7 minutes, and then we will share.

Reflection:

Students generally find that they are "experts" at more than they initially think. This is a good activity for they generally write more about what interests them. It also makes them feel good to write about what they know. In turn, I also find out interesting information about them that I might not know otherwise. I have, for example, read about students who are experts at hunting, coin collecting, bird calling, livestock showing, and surfing.

I Remember

Jeanne King
6th- and 7th-Grade Gifted and Talented Teacher,
Holt Middle School, Fayetteville, Arkansas

and

Joan Bennett
4th-Grade Teacher,
Holcomb Elementary School, Fayetteville, Arkansas

Directions:

Pass out folded "word cards," one to each person. Ask the writers *not* to look at the cards until directions are given. The cards should each have one of the following words on them: PLACE, PERSON, ACTIVITY, TIME, EXPERIENCE, or FEELING.

Next, say: *We are going to speak "I remembers." When it is time to begin, each of you will look at the word on your card and form a memory based on that word. Once we start, each person will say, "I remember," and finish that sentence with a memory. You may only provide one sentence. As soon as the person before you has finished his or her sentence, you are to say yours. This should proceed at a good pace. Put another way, there should be no break between the "I remembers." And there should be no comments either. We'll go around the room once in this way.*

OK, let's do this activity.

As you can see, our memories can be about a variety of topics. Keep that in mind when we begin to write in a few minutes. Also, remember how there was never a break between the "I remembers." Both of these ideas will be important as we do our quick write. We're going to try what we just did orally in writing. You will now take 3 minutes to write as many "I remembers" as you can. Remember, each memory must begin with "I remember," and as soon as you have finished your sentence, you should immediately begin to write "I remember" once again. Do this over and over again until the time is up. Your pencil cannot stop. You want your thoughts to flow. Your page might look like this. (Show a list of "I remember" sentences.)

You may begin.

Stop. Now, pick one "I remember" and write about it. Those who wish to share after we're done writing will be able to do so.

Reflection:

This exercise comes from the book *Wild Mind: Living the Writer's Life* by Natalie Goldberg. The purpose of the exercise is to force a flow of ideas where one idea leads to another in an expected or unexpected way. It is "mind-freeing" and can lead to surprises!

This quick write was used with fellow teachers and also in a third and fourth multigrade classroom. The reaction to the exercise was positive in both instances. As is often true with writing, the exercise brought back many poignant memories. The quick write seemed to promote honest, meaningful writing for each of the participants.

Sample from "I Remember" Exercise:

I remember Port Allen.
I remember riding in the station wagon.
I remember that purple dress I played ladies in.
I remember black patent leather shoes.
I remember white socks.
I remember neighbors next door.
I remember Peaches.
I remember that boy cutting off his finger.
I remember the circus in Baton Rouge.
I remember dancing even though I don't know how.
I remember wild hair.
I remember M.S.
I remember teaching with J.B.
I remember H. sleeping on the couch.
I remember singing in the choir.
I remember the art show at the airport.
I remember J. being so stupid.
I remember wearing B's ID bracelet.

REFERENCE

Goldberg, N. (1990). *Wild mind: Living the writer's life*. New York: Bantam Books.

Heaven on Earth

Lisa Darden
10th-, 11th-, and 12th-Grade English Teacher,
Van Buren High School, Van Buren, Arkansas

Directions:
First, share the following with your students: *In his book* The Five People You Meet in Heaven, *author Mitch Albom created a character known as "Blue Man," a blue-skinned sideshow freak at a seaside amusement park. Blue Man imparted the following bit of wisdom to the book's main character, Eddie: "People often belittle the place where they were born. But heaven can be found in the most unlikely corners." As the book progresses, Eddie discovers his various heavens on earth, including the following:*

- *The site where he first glimpsed his wife*
- *His modest childhood apartment*
- *His work site*
- *The local amusement park*
- *The bandshell where he first danced with his wife*
- *The fishing hole he cut into the pier*

Pondering where my own little pieces of heaven on earth are located, I came up with the following list, all places where I can go to escape from the hectic pace of life, all places to which I enjoy going:

- *The property I own on the bluff*
- *Aromas, the local coffee shop*
- *My truck on the highway with the music turned up loud*
- *A good book*
- *A close friend's house*
- *The cemetery where my ancestors are buried*
- *My bedroom*
- *The woods*
- *Somewhere quiet*

Over the past decade, my life has grown increasingly busy and compli-cated. Events like five job changes, a divorce, the loss of my mother, a move across the country, raising two children (one now a teenager) alone, caring for a disabled brother, and attempting to build a house have overrun my life. I have found that it is far too easy to get caught up in the rush of life and miss the good in life. Since vacations are few and far between, having my own piece of heaven on earth—a place to which I can escape, recuperate, recover, reconnect with my reason for being, and reemerge with a renewed spirit—has grown all the more important to my sanity. One such place that I like to escape is to Aroma's, a local coffee shop. Coincidentally, the name of my favorite drink at Aroma's is "Chocolate Heaven," a frozen mocha. When I need to slow it down a notch, I can always stroll into the shop, be greeted with a smile, and place my order. And it gets better. Drink in hand, I make my way to the back room where I can plop down into an overstuffed chair as I enjoy my "Chocolate Heaven." If I haven't brought something to read with me, I'll pick up the day's paper or a magazine to peruse. The atmosphere in the back room is very homey but with an added benefit: I'm not responsible for cleaning it. I love the colors of the walls. They are deep brown, a chocolate color. The walls are adorned with original artwork that changes frequently. You never know what quirky thing you'll find back there. A few minutes or a few hours lounging around the chocolate room at Aroma's with a "Chocolate Heaven" truly is a bit of heaven on earth for me.

Now ask your students the following questions: *Do you have such places in your own life—that is, a bit of heaven on earth? What places provide you with a sense of peace and fulfillment? Where are your pieces of heaven on earth and why?*

Have the students brainstorm in writing for about 4–5 minutes in order to create their own list of places.

Then ask the students to do the following: Choose one place on their list and expand on it. Tell them they have 5–7 minutes to write. After everyone has finished, ask for volunteers to share what they've written.

Reflection:

When I first read my piece, "Heaven on Earth," to my sophomore classes, I felt vulnerable. In my piece, I mentioned a number of events that have occurred in my life over the past several years, and I wondered if I had provided more information than was necessary, if I might lose some students with my "adult" worries, or if I was opening up too much to my students.

I was pleasantly surprised at how my students received the information. Heads didn't drop on the desks and students actually listened! When it came to their turn to write, I was even more pleasantly surprised at the lack of complaining; they actually seemed anxious to make their own lists and write their own paragraphs. Although the students didn't fall all over themselves to share their writing aloud (I could relate as I had just experienced similar trepidations myself), enough volunteered to make the activity work. Not only that, the students seemed to enjoy the assignment and sharing process.

Having since read Pat Schneider's *Writing Alone and With Others*, and discovering her point about the importance of the leader (teacher) modeling or writing with the participants (students), I believe the fact that I shared something I had written with the students made them more receptive to taking part in the initial activity. This tactic is certainly something worth considering for future classroom writing assignments.

One of the things I rediscovered while implementing the project was something I already knew well, not only from firsthand experience in my own writing, but also from teaching—and it is something I have emphasized repeatedly: "Write about what you know." Indeed, I believe the students enjoyed this writing because it was personal and something they knew well. It was not just an isolated project that required them to dream up something, but an activity to which they could relate. Indeed, I believe this was the reason they didn't complain or ask, "How long does it have to be?"

All in all, I believe the topic was well suited for the age group. Several students identified similar places as their little piece of heaven on earth (i.e., bedroom, secret fishing hole), and enjoyed discussing the topic. After hearing the students read from their selections and discuss different locales, I thought of several places to add to my own list. The assignment proved to be an exceptionally good writing and sharing experience.

REFERENCES

Albom, M. (2003). *The five people you meet in Heaven*. New York: Hyperion.
Schneider, P. (2002). *Writing alone and with others*. New York: Oxford University Press.

Darwin Awards!

Reagan Mauk
8th- and 9th-Grade English Teacher,
Central Junior High School, Springdale, Arkansas

Directions:

I have often wondered if there was a category for people who killed themselves with their own decisions. There are stories all over the nightly news discussing deaths of such idiotic proportions that one often wonders if they are, in fact, true. As it happens, there is just such a category for these "stupid" types of deaths. Having discovered that someone actually compiled lists of these events and declared them winners of a "Darwin Award," I wondered exactly what kind of deaths would qualify for a Darwin Award. I decided to investigate. Below is a fairly detailed explanation as to the type of individual who is most likely to be a recipient of a Darwin Award, as well as the list of "Rules and Eligibility" requirements taken from the book entitled *The Darwin Awards II* by Wendy Northcutt:

Darwin Awards commemorate those individuals who ensure the long-term survival of our species by removing themselves from the gene pool in a sublimely idiotic fashion. These [awards] are [given for] true accidental blunders that cost the hapless perpetrator his life. But don't mistake the intent of the humor. We are not poking tasteless fun at accidents. On the contrary! Darwin Awards poke fun at decisions that were obviously wrong at that time. In doing so, we celebrate examples of natural selection in action. We applaud those individuals who demonstrate the manifest unfitness of their genes by failing Life 101 in the 21st century.

The Darwin Awards … honor the not-so-unexpected demise of men who read fireworks' labels using a cigarette lighter. They are for those who eat from a bulging can, stand behind a running automobile, and kiss the contagious mouths of sick grandchildren. Darwin Awards are for people who repeatedly stump us with their cluelessness. And they are for those of us who somehow survived our own foolish risks. Remember those experiments with matches and plastic bottles, the fraying rope swing over the river, the jerry-built treehouse? Darwin Awards remind us how close we've come to winning an award ourselves.

Rules and Eligibility:

To qualify, nominees must improve the gene pool by eliminating themselves from the human race using astonishingly stupid means. Candidates are evaluated using the five rules of death, excellence, veracity, maturity, and self-selection.

1. The candidate must be eliminated from the gene pool. This means death or, less commonly, sterilization.

2. The candidate must show an astounding misapplication of common sense. Being hit by a falling safe is just bad luck. Pulling a safe downstairs, particularly while your shoelace is untied, is blatantly tempting fate—and being squashed by it is grounds for a Darwin.

3. The event must be verified. [For the purposes of a quick write, this is not necessary.]

4. The candidate must be capable of sound judgment. We're not talking about kids who imitate television stunt men, or adults addled by insulin shock. But if you choose to become inebriated and impair your own thinking, you can win a Darwin despite the self-inflicted infirmity.

5. The candidate must be the cause of his own death. One cannot have the greatness of a Darwin Award thrust upon oneself. Only a person who voluntarily throws caution to the wind, demonstrating his/her own manifest unfitness for survival, is worthy of this honor. (pp. 3–5)

After reading the explanation of the Darwin Awards and the rules, brainstorm for 2–3 minutes, compiling a list of at least 13 careers.

Next, tell the students the following: *Now choose one career and invent a way for someone in that vocation to receive a Darwin Award. Remember to follow the "Rules and Eligibility" requirements in describing your "Darwinian" death. You have 4–5 minutes to write.* Remember, keep it clean.

Have willing participants share.

Reflection:

My students and I have an immense amount of fun with this particular quick write. Students become very creative, and this lends itself well to journalistic writing. Both kids and adults seem to love coming up with horrifically stupid ways of killing oneself. If we have been spending a lot of time with very serious writing or reading, I'll pull this out for a tension-breaker. It does wonders for the classroom climate, and you get a good belly-laugh while you're at it.

REFERENCE

Northcutt, W. (2001). *The Darwin Awards II*. New York: Penguin.

MEMORIES

The Truth Will Set You Free

Charlene Holman
K–5 Title I Specialist,
Elmdale Elementary School, Springdale, Arkansas

Directions:

Read the story "The Little Notice" from *Chicken Soup for the Kid's Soul*. The story discusses a child's realization that honesty is the best policy. Upon reading the story, have the students remember a time when the lesson of honesty was brought home for them. Allow students to share their memories briefly to help them get their thoughts organized. Give the students about 5 minutes to write freely about their past experience with learning an honesty lesson. When time is called, allow a few of the students to share their stories.

Variation:

Instead of reading the story "The Little Notice," a story can be told that demonstrates the value of honesty.

Spark the Brain, Ignite the Pen: Quick Writes for Kindergarten Through High School Teachers and Beyond, 2nd Edition, pp. 35–52
Copyright © 2009 by Information Age Publishing

REFERENCE

Thompson, K. (1998). The little notice. In J. Canfield, M. V. Hansen, P. Hansen, & I. Dunlap (Eds.), *Chicken soup for the kid's soul: 101 stories of courage, hope, and laughter* (pp. 343–344). Deerfield Beach, FL: Health Communications.

A Matter of Choice

Lory Conrad
11th- and 12th-Grade English Teacher,
Hackett High School, Hackett, Arkansas

Directions:

To begin, ask students to list choices they have made that day. Most will be of the trivial sort, such as what to eat for breakfast, what to wear to school, and so on. Discuss how we each make countless choices every day. Some of them are trivial and are made almost unconsciously. Others are more serious and may even have long-term consequences. Introduce Robert Frost's poem, "The Road Not Taken," and explain to students that it is about making a choice that has long-term consequences. Read the poem to the students. Then tell the students they have 5 minutes to write a response, and in doing so they may choose to write about a choice they have made that has "made all the difference" in their lives. Or, tell them they may wish to write about a difficult decision they have had to make, or a decision they would make differently if they had it to do over again.

Reflection:

Making the "right" choices and accepting the consequences of such is a major issue in the lives of my senior high students. Unfortunately, some of them have already learned the hard way about making bad choices. This activity sometimes serves as a springboard for my students' personal narratives or memoirs. It has also been a starting point for some of their persuasive essays in which they urge others not to make the same mistakes they have made.

REFERENCE

Frost, R. (2000). The road not taken. In *Robert Frost: Three books* (p. 119). Ann Arbor, MI: Lowe & B. Hould.

Even Sick Days Have Good Memories

Kimberly McGrath
ESL Teacher,
Jones Elementary School, Springdale, Arkansas

Directions:

Before this quick write, you will need the following: (1) Paper and pencils for the writers to use; (2) a comforting object from your childhood; and (3) *The Sick Day* written by Patricia MacLachlan and illustrated by Jane Dyer. This is a warm and loving book about a little girl named Emily. She has a lot of personality, but today she is staying home because she is sick. Her dad is willing to try everything to get her to feel better. This will likely remind the reader of comforting rituals, tender care, and special times that affected his or her own sick days as a child.

Start the quick write by sharing the object you brought from your childhood. Then ask the students if they had a special object when they were small that was comforting, or have a special memory of an action from a family member. Let a few students share something that comes to mind. Then tell them that you are going to read *The Sick Day*, and when you are finished, you are going to ask them to write about anything the story brought to mind. Give everyone 3–5 minutes to write. Finally, ask for volunteers to share their writing with the group.

Reflection:

People of all ages, literally kindergarten children to adults, love this story. It usually makes people think about special memories with a parent, or an object that was special to them as a child. The book usually makes people smile at one another and results in spirited comments about favorite memories. Bringing an object of your own seems to give the students permission to talk about any object, no matter how old or embarrassing. Even that special bear with pen marks and no eyes becomes endearing and valuable to the "older" or cooler students, and one student's comment often triggers another student's memory of things he or she had forgotten. I love reading this, and I know you will too.

REFERENCE

MacLachlan, P. (1999). *The sick day*. New York: Random House.

Have You Ever Had One of Those Days?

Karen J. Edwards
7th-Grade English Teacher,
McNair Middle School, Fayetteville, Arkansas

Directions:

Read *Alexander and the Terrible, Horrible, No Good, Very Bad Day* by Judith Viorst, a story about a little boy who has what he considers the "worst day ever." Instruct the students to write about their worst day—real or imagined!

Reflection:

The reaction to this quick write has always been extremely favorable. Almost everyone has had one very bad day, and both kids and adults seem to love to share it! Sometimes, if we are having a particularly rough day at school, I will pull this quick write out on the spur of the moment and do it with my class. Typically, the "worst day," laced with humor, allows our classroom to fill with laughter.

REFERENCE

Viorst, J. (1972). *Alexander and the terrible, horrible, no good, very bad day.* New York: Macmillan.

Ira Sleeps Over

Mary Wince
Coordinator of Gifted Education,
Valley Springs School, Valley Springs, Arkansas

Directions:

Think about the very first time you went to a sleepover. How did you feel? (For students who have not yet experienced a sleepover, ask them to imagine how they would feel going to their first one.) *In today's book, Ira has been invited to spend the night with Reggie, his best friend in the whole world. As I read* Ira Sleeps Over, *think about how Ira's feelings change throughout the story.*

(After reading, ask students to briefly recall Ira's feelings. Discuss why Ira can't make up his mind about taking his teddy bear.)

Now it's your turn. Write about your first sleepover and how you felt (or about a time when you felt worried or write about one of your favorite toys). You will have 5 minutes to write.

After the time expires, invite authors to share.

Reflection:

After the initial quick write, I often return to the story and ask students to recall Reggie's plans for the sleepover. I return to the text and reread page 16: *"Tonight," he [Reggie] said, "when you come to my house, we are going to have fun, fun, fun. First, I'll show you my junk collection. And after that we'll have a wrestling match. And after that, a pillow fight. And after that we'll do a magic trick. And after that we'll play checkers. And after that we'll play dominoes. And after that we can fool around with my magnifying glass."*

Now it's your turn. Imagine you are planning a sleepover with your very best friend. Write what you would do to have fun, fun, fun. You will have 3–5 minutes to write.

After writing, I ask each student to star two favorite ideas and then share one with the group. We write a group story with each student contributing one idea.

Reflection:

Students love beginning every line with, "And after that." And Reggie's pattern of speech provides a great opportunity for a mini-lesson on author's craft. Though we usually don't begin each sentence in the same way or with the word *and*, Bernard Waber chooses to write this way so that we know how excited Reggie is and just how he sounds when he talks. As an added bonus, emergent readers find the repetitive beginnings of each sentence in the group story easy to read.

This quick write is especially appropriate for students in the primary grades.

REFERENCE

Waber, B. (1972). *Ira sleeps over.* Boston: Houghton Mifflin.

Dead Poets Society

Mary Wince
Coordinator of Gifted Education,
Valley Springs School, Valley Springs, Arkansas

Directions:

As we view this clip of Dead Poets Society, *which focuses on the first day of classes at a boys' preparatory school, think about the way Mr. Keating, the new English instructor, introduces himself to his students.*

(Show the "first day of classes" clip, which is about 10 minutes into the film, beginning with the chiming of the clock tower and the boys climbing the stairwell. Continue viewing for approximately 6-1/2 minutes and conclude with Mr. Keating's challenge to his students.)

Then suggest one or more of the following possibilities to your students: *On the first day of classes, Mr. Keating whispers a challenge to his students: "Carpe diem. Seize the day boys. Make your lives extraordinary." What will be your legacy? How will you make your life extraordinary?*

Write about a teacher who has had a positive (or negative) impact on your life.

Reflection:

Although *Dead Poets Society* is rated PG, this particular clip is appropriate for students in grades 6 and up. The movie in its entirety is more appropriate for grades 8–12. The clip is ideal for provoking students to think about what their goals in life are and/or those teachers that have had an impact on their lives.

(Note: This is a "must-see" movie for educators.)

REFERENCE

Henderson, D. (Producer), & Weir, P. (Director). (1989). *Dead poets society* [Film]. Touchstone Pictures.

Any Great Aunts Out There?

Janis Gibson
Literacy Specialist,
OUR Educational Co-Op, Harrison, Arkansas

Directions:

Begin by reminiscing or telling a short memory of a favorite relative, friend, or teacher. Give a little background about the person and why he or she is your favorite. Then read *My Great-Aunt Arizona* by Gloria Houston. This story tells the life story of the author's aunt who was a teacher at a one-room schoolhouse and how she touched the lives and minds of every child she taught. Following the story, have participants write about their favorite relative, friend, or teacher.

Reflection:

This activity allows participants the time to search their minds for important people who have made a difference in their lives, whether it was a relative, friend, or teacher. It allows the writer to assess what made (makes) that person important to them and the characteristics of the person that set him or her apart from others in their lives. The results are often quite powerful, and, at least with older students, emotional.

REFERENCE

Houston, G. (1993). *My great-aunt Arizona*. New York: Scholastic.

A Most Unforgettable Character

Samuel Totten
Director of the Northwest Arkansas Writing Project,
University of Arkansas, Fayetteville

Directions:

I simply start out by telling a story: *We've all met someone in life who we find particularly fascinating—either because of their experiences, their joy for life, their unique personality, or their flare for the unusual. I've been lucky in that I've met lots of characters over the years, but one I met early on in life—I was about 13 years old or so—was a person named Mrs. Dietrich. She was an old lady, about 70 or so—actually she looked ancient to my young eyes—who lived in a nondescript little wooden house surrounded by an overgrown and messy yard. If you looked at her on the street she was so common-looking you wouldn't give her a second glance. But enter her home and listen to her stories and I assure you, never would forget her.*

On her walls she had snowshoes that she used when she and her husband lived in the Yukon and were both sheriffs. Next to the snowshoes was an old-fashioned pistol in a scuffed-up leather holster cracked with age. Spread across the tables in her house were bows and arrows she had actually taken away from Native Americans (she didn't call them that, as the phrase had not been invented yet, and thus she called them Indians or by their tribal name) she had arrested on the frontier. Her sink was full of what looked like weeds, but they were plants that grew wild in her yard and that she said were healthy for you and that she ate as a regular part of her diet.

She was forever complaining about how television was so fake and that all of the westerns and cowboy shows treated the Native Americans as if they were little better than clowns. She said she had written scores of letters to the movie studios berating them for using the wrong clothing, feathers, bonnets, and homes for the Native Americans in their TV shows and movies.

I could go on and on, but I know that you also have stories to tell about the most unforgettable character you've ever met. Take 5 minutes and write about that person, using "showing, not telling" language.

Reflection:

I have used this quick write with students from fifth grade through graduate school, and most students at the various levels have enjoyed the activity. It often brings back a memory of someone they, in one way or another, cherish the thought of but often do not think about. The pieces are often quite vivid, and it is difficult to cut the sharing off at 3–6 minutes.

Remembering Relatives

Penny Bradley
4th-Grade Teacher,
Garfield Elementary School, Garfield, Arkansas

Directions:

Initially, for quite young children at least, one should review with students the term "relatives," and brainstorm some examples. Next, one should read *The Relatives Came* by Cynthia Rylant, a story about a group of relatives on a summer vacation.

After the story has been read, ask the students to close their eyes and think for a minute about a special memory that includes one or more of their relatives. Then ask the students to write about the memory that has come to mind.

Reflection:

The Relatives Came is a good selection for helping students recall special memories associated with their relatives. Students love the opportunity to write about family members and the events that surround them. This book is lighthearted and fun to share. It generally triggers funny stories and happy memories for the students. This quick write is a good way to learn interesting tidbits about individual students during the first few weeks of school.

REFERENCE

Rylant, C. (1985). *The relatives came.* New York: Bradbury Press.

Dancing Memories

Trudy Honson
2nd-Grade Writing Specialist,
Jones Elementary School, Springdale, Arkansas

Directions:

I am going to read you a story called The Dance *by Richard Paul Evans. This book is about a father who watches his daughter dance through various stages of her life. It is very emotional and easily lends itself to self-reflection in regard to our relationship with our own fathers or special people who have touched our lives.* (Note: Tissues may be required.)

As the book is being read, memories of your own life may start to replay in your mind. As they do, I want you to think about that special memory that this book creates for you.

Read the book *The Dance* by Richard Paul Evans.

Now, please write about a special memory that this book has triggered in your mind. It does not have to be about your own father, but it certainly can be.

Reflection:

The Dance was read at a workshop I attended, and we were asked to respond to a special memory about our fathers. The writing that was created was very emotional and moving. I modified the original response for my own class to any special memory that the book created because a lot of our students do not have fathers in their lives.

REFERENCE

Evans, R. P. (1999). *The dance*. New York: Simon & Schuster.

All the Places to Love

Mary Wince
Coordinator of Gifted Education,
Valley Springs School, Valley Springs, Arkansas

Directions:

I introduce this quick write in the following manner: *Each of us has a special place to call our own. Perhaps it's the view from the back porch, a favorite restaurant, or a special spot on the river, creek, or ocean side. Maybe it's a destination we've visited in our travels or a place from our childhood—the gym where we played ball or cheered for our team, a high school hangout, or the home of a close relative. In today's book,* All the Places to Love, *we'll meet Eli and his family. Everyone in Eli's family has a favorite place. As I read, notice the ways in which the author Patricia MacLachlan uses sensory details to describe all the places to love.* (After reading, ask students to recall sensory details from the story.)

Now it's your turn. Write about a place close to your heart. Take us there through your writing. Remember to use sensory details to describe the place you love. You will have 5 minutes to write. (After the time expires, invite authors to share.)

Reflection:

Students in Grades 5–12 have little difficulty incorporating sensory details in this quick write. If students respond in narrative form, encourage them to consider rewriting in a different genre, such as poetry.

REFERENCE

MacLachlan, P. (1994). *All the places to love.* New York: Dutton.

Treasured Treasures

Brenda Marks
3rd-Grade Literacy Teacher,
Jones Elementary School, Springdale, Arkansas

Directions:

The story, *Lilly's Purple Plastic Purse*, by Kevin Henke, is about a little girl who loves everything about school, especially her teacher, Mr. Slinger. One day she brings her new purple plastic purse to school for show-and-tell, but Mr. Slinger says she has to wait until the end of the day to share it. She doesn't like this idea and makes a very bad choice. The result is having the purse taken by the teacher and not getting to share it.

When I read this story, I started thinking about those things in my life that are precious to me. In particular, I have a set of blue porcelain candleholders that belonged to my grandmother. My uncle brought them to her when he returned from England during World War II. I remember them sitting on a shelf in her dining room. When she died, my family and I went in her house and took those things that were precious to each of us. Those were the first two things that I quickly gathered up before anyone else could get to them. I had admired them while I was growing up, heard the stories behind them, and saw them adorn her table at family gatherings. To me, those candleholders were something that I wanted to keep in my family. Someday, I will pass them on to my daughter for her family to enjoy.

After reading the story to the class, ask them to reflect upon things that stand out as being genuine treasures to them. Ask the students to think about personal items that are so precious and valued that they would never want to part with them. Ask them to make a list of those items. Give students a few minutes to think about which one of those items is the absolute most precious treasure that they own. Tell them to imagine that someone wants to take it away to help them decide which one is the one that they just can't part with.

After the students decide on a particular item, ask them to write about it. Tell them to describe the item, why it is so important to them, where they got it, and why it is such a treasured treasure.

After writing, let students who wish to share their writing with the class in the author's chair.

Reflection:

I have used this exercise with first and third graders, but it could easily be adapted for use with older students. The quality of writing will vary depending on the age group. My first graders chose items like their bikes, their dolls, or their Nintendo game players. A few third graders went a little more in depth and chose things like books or jewelry given to them on special occasions. Some students gave vivid descriptions and heartfelt reasons why those items were treasured. My lower-level students gave more vague descriptions and did not support their chosen item as fully. After teaching this the first time, I began to model my own writing about the candleholders on chart paper to give them a clearer idea of what I was looking for. We circled words that described the item, why it was important, and where it came from so they could see the details. Then we circled the words that supported why I felt this was my most treasured treasure. This helped them to see more clearly how the parts would fit together and have more meaning for the reader.

REFERENCE

Henke, K. (1996). *Lilly's purple plastic purse*. New York: Greenwillow Books.

Do You Speak My Language?

Lacinda Files
*3rd-Grade Writing Teacher and District Literacy Specialist,
Jones Elementary School, Springdale, Arkansas*

Directions:

Read aloud the picture book *Josepha* by Jim McGugan. Pause, show, and enjoy the incredible illustrations. Josepha tells the story of an immigrant boy who comes to America at the turn of the twentieth century along with his "city" family. The family struggles to make it as farmers and to learn the language of their new land. At school Josepha is forced to sit with the little children because he either can't or won't learn the strange new tongue. Josepha does, however, find a new friend, and he shares a part of himself with his new friend and with his teacher, whom the book simply calls "Miss." Josepha is a touching tale of tough choices that families must often make for economic reasons. It highlights various differences between cultures as well as language barriers, which pervade many schools. More important, in my opinion, is the book's theme of companionship, friendship, and sharing.

Think about the best, but greatest gift anyone has ever given you. The gift need not be expensive to be precious. In fact, something used or "homemade" is often more valuable than a "store-bought" gift. Consider the person who gave you the precious gift. Did he or she sacrifice anything so that you might have something? Perhaps your gift is not something you can see just yet, such as money being put aside for a college education or a car for when you turn 16. Take a few minutes and write about the best, greatest, or most sacrificial gift anyone has ever given you.

Reflection:

I purchased *Josepha—A Prairie Boys' Story* and fell in love with it because the story appealed to me, as did the illustrations. I love the story because of its country setting, but also because it speaks to me the way my students speak to me every day! So many of them come to school knowing little or no English and are thrown into a world of "sheep talk," where adults flail their arms and point and smile and try to communicate with them and in the end do very little in the way of communicating much of anything. Josepha and his friend manage to speak to one another most clearly through the acts of giving, sharing, and caring.

REFERENCE

McGugan, J. (1994). *Josepha—A prairie boy's story.* San Francisco: Chronicle Books.

Remembering?

Rita Caver
10th-Grade Honors English,
Fayetteville High School, Fayetteville, Arkansas

Directions:

Read *Wilfrid Gordon McDonald Partridge* by Mem Fox. Then, ask the students to share aloud the areas (or types) of memory that the old folks told Wilfrid (e.g., something warm, something from long ago, something that makes you cry, etc.).

Next, say: *Think about the items that you could put away that would help you spark your memory some time in the distant future. For each of the areas, write about the item that you would pick. Tell about its significance.*

After writing for 5 minutes, share.

Reflection:

It would be fun to have younger students actually bring in their items for show-and-tell as they read their written work. For social studies, students could write this from the point of view of a historical figure. Another idea is to have them write about the specific items they might choose to represent a particular historical period.

REFERENCE

Fox, M. (1995). *Wilfrid Gordon McDonald Partridge*. La Jolla, CA: Kane/Miller.

What Is Your Literacy Autobiography?

Janis Gibson
Literacy Specialist,
OUR Educational Co-op, Harrison, Arkansas

Directions:

Eudora Welty's book, *One Writer's Beginnings*, begins with the chapter "Listening." Beginning with page 1 to the break on page 9, there are numerous references to the rich literature background that was present in her home. Pick as many passages as you need to engage your students with stories of her early experiences with literature and read them aloud to your group. (Personally, I particularly liked parts that described the "library," her father's childhood book, places to read in her house, and the importance of the alphabet.)

Following the reading, have participants reflect a moment on their own literacy background. Here, it's a good idea for the teacher to share key moments in her or his "literacy autobiography" so that the students gain an even deeper understanding of what such a "work" entails. In some cases, a teacher may wish to have his or her students brainstorm ideas (e.g., favorite authors, favorite books, first time something was written for fun, favorite genre of writing, etc.).

Next, have the students write their "Literacy Autobiography."

Reflection:

I first used this activity with a group of Northwest Arkansas Writing Project teacher consultants. Everyone seemed to enjoy the activity and shared openly the aspects of their literacy autobiographies. I feel this is a good activity to set the atmosphere for any writing session—be it the classroom, a writers' retreat, or an inservice. It definitely gets everyone thinking.

REFERENCE

Welty, E. (1984). Listening. In *One writer's beginnings* (pp. 1–39). Cambridge, MA: Harvard University Press.

Bowl After Bowl of Chicken Soup

Clare Lesieur
4th-Grade Teacher,
Skyline Heights Elementary School, Harrison, Arkansas

Directions:

Chicken Soup for the Kid's Soul *is a collection of 101 stories. Famous people have written some of these stories about their childhoods, but kids just like you have written many of them, too. Some of the stories are sad, and some of them are funny. But most importantly, all of them are true! This kind of writing about real-life experiences is called personal narrative.*

Throughout the school year, I will pick up this book and read a story to you. As I read, you may jot down any connections you make between the story and your life. After I finish reading, you will have about 5 minutes to begin your own personal narrative about anything the story makes you think of.

Select a story and read it to the class. Give students time to write and then share.

Reflection:

I have used this book for numerous quick writes. My students seem to really connect to the stories on an emotional level. The topics are of special interest to kids (e.g., love, friendship, family, death, etc.), and the personal narrative is a form they appreciate. (Students enjoy writing about themselves!) *Chicken Soup for the Kid's Soul* is aimed at children ages 9–12.

There are many *Chicken Soup* books, including ones for preteens and teenagers.

REFERENCE

Canfield, J., Hansen, M. V., Hansen, P., & Dunlap, I. (Eds.) (1998). *Chicken soup for the kid's soul*. Deerfield Beach, FL: Health Communications.

Don't Worry, Be Happy

Anna Gawf
2nd-Grade Teacher,
Thurman G. Smith Elementary School, Springdale, Arkansas

Directions:

We all have worries, and Wemberly, the main character from Kevin Henkes' book, *Wemberly Worried*, is no exception. Wemberly, the classic worrywart, literally worries about everything. School is fast approaching, and her fear of attending school for the first time is by far her greatest worry. When Wemberly meets a new friend at school, she suddenly doesn't have as many worries.

To begin the quick write, ask the students if they have ever worried. Introduce the title and author of the book *Wemberly Worried*, and explain that the main character, a mouse named Wemberly, worries about everything all the time. Read pages 1–21. Briefly discuss how the author uses humor to show that excessive worrying can be silly. Instruct the audience to take a moment to think about something that is silly to worry about. Tell the audience they will have 3–5 minutes to respond to the following prompt: "It's ridiculous to worry about …" After 5 minutes, ask the audience to stop writing. Ask for volunteers to share their writing.

Reflection:

A teacher can if he or she wishes read only a portion of the book. With my students, however, I read the entire book. I then prompt students to write about a time they were particularly worried or about something they are currently worried about. All of the students were drawn to the humor and illustrations of the book. They could easily relate to Wemberly's worries, particularly the first-day-of-school jitters. The beginning of the school year provides the perfect opportunity to read and write with this book.

This quick write has served as a great launching pad for my students, as many have chosen to develop their quick writes into longer pieces.

REFERENCE

Henkes, K. (2000). *Wemberly worried*. Hong Kong: Greenwillow Books.

SELF-DISCOVERY

What I Know

Samuel Totten
*Founder and Director of the Northwest Arkansas Writing Project,
and Professor of Curriculum and Instruction,
University of Arkansas, Fayetteville*

Directions:

I start by saying: *It's often interesting to note those things that one truly knows in life. Actually, it's also interesting to note what one does not know for sure—for example, in my case, exactly how human beings detect different smells and scents and why.*

Anyhow, I've come up with a list of things that I definitely know based on my 40-odd years of experience as a human being on planet Earth, and I would like to share some of them with you. (Note: Here, each teacher should read his or her own list of "I knows"):

1. I know it is difficult to follow Socrates's dictum, "Know thyself."

2. I know I am most comfortable in the ocean—way out in the ocean just floating or surfing huge, glassy waves.

Spark the Brain, Ignite the Pen: Quick Writes for Kindergarten Through High School Teachers and Beyond, 2nd Edition, pp. 53–74

3.   I know I am lucky to have my wife for my wife.
4.   I know that I will always miss my dog Rocky, who died two years ago.
5.   I know I have a lot to learn still about being a superb educator.
6.   I know I am adamantly against nuclear power.
7.   I know I am in favor of alternative, clean sources of energy.
8.   I know I will never smoke a cigarette.
9.   I know, unequivocally, that secondhand smoke is dangerous to one's health.
10. I know that as long as the state of Germany exists, it will be stained with the blood of the Holocaust.
11. I know that genocide is not likely in most cases to be prevented until we solve the problem of *realpolitik* and an absence of "political will" by the powers that be.
12. I know that my graduate education at Columbia University was special.
13. I know the power of writing to help one explore who he or she is.
14. I know the power of writing to learn.
15. I know that those of us who are advocates of writing to learn have a long, long way to go to reach our goal of its becoming an integral part of every school's curriculum.
16. I know that I detest mediocrity.
17. I know that I am obsessed with the concept of immortality.
18. I know that Paul Celan, T.S. Eliot, Samuel Coleridge, and Dylan Thomas are among my favorite poets.
19. I know that everyone across the globe deserves the protection of his or her basic human rights.
20. I know that I need to be more altruistic.
21. I know that the use of the term "ethnic cleansing" is often a cop-out and a euphemism for genocide.
22. I know I am obsessed with the crime of genocide.
23. I know that we do not know half of what our government does in our name.
24. I know that the United States has supported murderous dictators in the name of *realpolitik*.
25. I know that I am responsible for my own thoughts, feelings, and actions.

Next, I say: *OK, now I'd like to have you write down your list of "I knows." In the next couple of minutes try to get down as many as you can. Be sure to begin each statement with I know and be absolutely sure that each statement is as true as it can be.*

Ask if anyone would like to share a portion (**5–7 items,** *only*) of his or her list. Allow time for three or four people to share.

Now I wish to have you select one "I know sentence" and write a narrative in which you convey your most honest thoughts about that which you know.

Write along with the rest of the group.

Ask if anyone wishes to share.

Reflection:

This is an extremely powerful activity to use with students from about fourth grade up. Younger students may focus on concrete topics such as school subjects, sports, television shows, or pop stars, whereas older students invariably move into more philosophical realms. It is an excellent activity to help students become more reflective about their own lives.

(Note: *Only when using this with educators:* Ask how this could be used in particular disciplines for writing-to-learn purposes.)

Art, Like Morality, Consists of Drawing the Line Somewhere!

Mike Thomas
5th-Grade Teacher,
Washington Elementary, Fayetteville, Arkansas

Directions:

I place the following statement on the overhead or blackboard:

Morality (a definition): Relating to principles of
right and wrong behavior. Relating to or acting on
the mind, character, or will. Sanctioned by one's
conscience or ethical judgment.

Then I say: *We, adults, are constantly teaching kids moral lessons. "Who you really are is how you act when no one is watching," we say. "Do the right thing!" we advise. "What is the moral of that story?" we ask.*

Morality is a difficult thing to dictate or control in people, but if you open your mind and become self-aware for a moment you might find out something about yourself.

I want you to imagine you are a newspaper salesperson, and you manage 25 different paper machines. Lately people have been putting their 50 cents in and taking more than one paper, and this has drastically cut into your profits.

You have devised three signs, but which one will be the most effective? The signs read as follows:

1. *"You are under surveillance. If you take more than what you have paid for you will be arrested and/or fined." (Fear of being caught)*

2. *"This is how I make my living; please don't take more than you have paid for." (A sense of community)*

3. *Stealing is a crime! What kind of person are you?" (Individual reflection)*

I want you to write a quick response by choosing what you think the most effective sign for the majority of society would be, and tell why you think so. Then note which sign would mean the most to you and tell why. Which words carry the most weight for you? Why?

Reflection:

I have used this quick write with fifth graders, and it is rather astonishing how reflective the students get when considering the above questions. This is an activity that not only gets the students writing, but reflecting on the responsibilities people have in society and the type of individuals they are at this juncture in their young lives.

A Gift From the Heart

Samuel Totten
***Founder and Director of the Northwest Arkansas Writing Project,
and Professor of Curriculum and Instruction,
University of Arkansas, Fayetteville***

Read O'Henry's *Gift of the Magi* to the students (it's only about two and a half pages long). Then, without any discussion, have the students write a story when either they or someone they knew gave something extremely precious they owned to someone else out of great admiration and/or love.

Or, if students have never given such a gift they can write about their being a recipient of such a gift. Note: If students have never given such a gift or been a recipient of one, then they should be given the opportunity to write about a person who they would one day give such a gift to and why—and, if they have any idea as to what such a gift would be they should be encouraged to mention it and comment on why they would choose that particular gift.

Reflection

"Gift of the Magi" is a story that most students—no matter how immature or jaded they are—will never forget. Responding to the story in a quick write is also likely to be an experience that stays with them a long time—that is, the essence of what they wrote, and why.

REFERENCE

O'Henry. (2003). *The gift of the Magi and other stories*. New York: Scholastic.

Examining One's Life

Samuel Totten
*Founder and Director of the Northwest Arkansas Writing Project,
and Professor of Curriculum and Instruction,
University of Arkansas, Fayetteville*

Directions:

The teacher should write the following on the board or overhead:

"The Unexamined Life is Not Worth Living" —Socrates

and

"Know Thyself" —Socrates

Next, the teacher should say: *Please select one of these statements by Socrates, the famous ancient Greek philosopher, and discuss either the significance the statement has for each and every individual **or** its significance for you as a human being. In doing so, try to provide specific examples/moments from your own life.*

OR, conversely,

Say: *Reflect in writing on the meaning of one of the two statements, agreeing or disagreeing with it. State why you agree or disagree, and then comment on how you could possibly use the message inherent in the statement to help guide your own life journey.*

Reflection:
This is an excellent quick write to use in an English, history, social studies or government classroom for the students' responses can be used as a segue to examine how such statements apply to various literary characters and/or historical/political figures.

Note:
I've found that many university students at the sophomore and junior levels have difficulty even understanding the most basic notion of Socrates statement "The Unexamined Life is Not Worth Living." Thus, if teachers provide this statement as one of the options, they may need to take a couple of minutes to discuss with the students the essence of what Socrates was getting at in making such an assertion.

It Is All in the Eye of the Beholder

Samuel Totten
***Founder and Director of the Northwest Arkansas Writing Project,
and Professor of Curriculum and Instruction,
University of Arkansas, Fayetteville***

Directions:
The teacher should begin by relating a true story as to how two different people he/she knows view the same scene, object, food, or "being" (such as a mammal, insect or reptile) with "totally different eyes," and thus "totally different perspectives. For example, whenever I passed an oil refinery in California, Texas or New Jersey I always mused how the tangle of grimy pipes, cylinders, vats, furnaces, holding tanks and so on and so forth were interesting but ugly and smelly. My father-in-law, an executive for Mobil Oil and an engineer, on the other hand, had what seemed like a love affair with oil refineries. Indeed, they were a thing of beauty to him;

so much so, there were few places in the world where he was more content than in the middle of a oil refinery.

Next, the teacher should say and do: *OK, what I'm going to do is provide each of you with a series of pictures/photographs. As you will see, each set of photographs (each set is comprised of two photographs) is exactly the same except for the captions on each of the photographs. That is, for example, one of the photographs will have a positive word describing it while the other photograph (which, again, is a photograph of the very same thing) will have a negative word describing it, e.g., frightening/fascinating; ugly/beautiful; wise/old; immature/joyful.*

Once you receive your set of cards (each student needs to receive a set of cards) *examine your photos. Once you've done that you can do any of the following: select the photography you like best with the caption you most agree with and write why you feel that way about the photograph/picture. Or, you may write why you think/believe/feel that the scene, item, animal is beautiful (or conversely, ugly). Or, if you wish, you may write about both items, comparing and contrasting your thoughts as to why and how different individuals would perceive that very same object, scene, being as ugly and beautiful. You have five minutes to write a quick response.*

Once everyone has completed a rough draft those who wish to share may do so.

Reflection:

I actually came up with this idea for a quick write as I was walking through Heathrow Airport several years ago on my way from the United States to Rwanda. Along a long corridor were a series of pairs of photographs and on one photo of the pair was a negative response in writing and on the other was a positive response. It automatically made one think about a host of issues: one's own take on the world, stereotypes and how easy one buys into them, the critical difference between seeing a glass as half full or half empty, and so on and so forth.

I have used this with students in an English class to, ultimately, address the power of stereotypes and I have used it with students in a social studies class to examine one's perspective on the world (again, something often related to stereotypes) and how different people view the world.

Living Life for All Its Worth

Samuel Totten
Founder and Director of the Northwest Arkansas Writing Project,
and Professor of Curriculum and Instruction,
University of Arkansas, Fayetteville

Directions:

Put the following excerpt from Nikos Kazantzakis' novel *Zorba the Greek* —in which Zorba is speaking to a friend on how different people look at life—on the overhead, and read it to the students.

> "One day I had gone to a little village. An old grandfather of ninety was busy planting an almond tree. 'What granddad?' I exclaimed. 'Planting an almond tree?' And he, bent as he was, turned round and said 'My son, I carry on as if I should never die.' I replied: 'And I carry on as if I was going to die any minute.' Which of us was right, boss?"

Ask the students to do one of two things: Select the stance that he or she is most in tune with in regard to his/her worldview of life or come up with a different metaphor on seeing life. In both cases, students should be asked to provide a rationale for his/her choice/position.

Reflection:

This quick write is ideal for encouraging students to reflect on how they look at life and why. Not only is it a good reflective activity for young people to engage in, but this activity can be tied to virtually any piece of literature in order to "prompt" students to begin to examine the world view of the character(s) they are reading about.

REFERENCE

Kazantzakis, N. (1961). *Zorba the Greek*. London: Faber and Faber.

My Achilles' Heel

Samuel Totten
*Founder and Director of the Northwest Arkansas Writing Project,
and Professor of Curriculum and Instruction,
University of Arkansas, Fayetteville*

Directions:

Relate the following to your students: *The story of Achilles is an interesting one. Achilles, the Greek god, was a great and brave warrior who won all of his battles handily. However, in one battle he was struck, of all places, in the heel of his foot. It just so happened that that spot was his most vulnerable; thus, after being speared there, he perished. From that Greek myth comes the notion of the "Achilles' Heel." Today we use that term to refer to a person's greatest vulnerability or weakness—one that may not be obvious to the naked eye but is very real; indeed, one that can have a tremendous impact on an individual's life.*

It is important to note that everyone—no matter how rich, famous, handsome, beautiful or intelligent—has an Achilles' heel. Some may think that a person has the perfect life and no vulnerable spots or flaws at all. But that is not true. Every single person has an Achilles' heel—the highest religious figure, the most respected politician, the greatest military officer, the richest business person, the most famous movie star or rock star. Some, though, recognize they have such a vulnerability and weakness and seek to compensate for it and/or overcome it. Others may allow the vulnerability to overcome them and affect their lives in certain negative ways.

Among some of the many Achilles' heels of rich and famous people have been the following: extreme shyness (the Academy Award-winning actor, Dustin Hoffman); drug abuse (actor Robert Downey Jr.); jealousy (Paris Hilton over the fact that her best friend Nichole Richey got engaged); believing and acting as if he were above the law (former U.S. President Richard M. Nixon, Saddam Hussein, and Michael Jackson); a hair-trigger temper (General George Patton). Note: Teachers may wish to replace and insert different names and examples here (e.g., those their students may find more germane to their interests).

Among other types of Achilles' heels include an almost crippling lack of self-confidence; greed; selfishness; arrogance; prejudice; a propensity for foul language and/or lewd behavior; being overly concerned with what others think.

In the next 5-8 minutes I want you to think about your own Achilles' heel and write about it. In doing so, provide some classic examples as to how that weakness of yours has affected your life in concrete ways. You may also write about how you have attempted to come to terms with your Achilles' Heel so that it does not negatively impact your life.

Reflection:
More often than not, most people do not want to really focus on their major weaknesses in life. It's either too painful or embarrassing to do so or its easier to focus on the positive versus the negative. But there is a real value in focusing on one's weaknesses, for until one recognizes such one is not likely to begin to address it. This is a great exercise to use in an English classroom when studying literature about individuals who are not as reflective as they could or should be (everyone from Tom Sawyer to Alfred J. Prufrock and from Bigger Thomas to Willie Stark).

Introducing a New Me

Clare Lesieur
4th-Grade Teacher,
Skyline Heights Elementary School, Harrison, Arkansas

Directions:
The beginning of the school year is an exciting time for all of us. In the poem, "Introducing a New Me," Dakos writes about a student's goals for the new school year.

Read the poem, and ask the students to write about the person they want to be this year. They may write in poetic or narrative form. After 5 minutes of writing time, allow students to introduce their "new selves."

Introducing a New Me
There's a new ME this year,
An on-time ME,
A clean-desk ME,
A first-to-hand-in-assignments ME,
A listens-in-class-to-the-teacher ME,
A teacher's-pet-for-the-first-time-in-my-life ME,
An always-willing-to-be-good-and-help-out ME,
A dead-serious-get-the-work-done-and-hand-it-in-
before-it's-due ME.
The problem is
The new ME
Is not like ME
At all.

Reflection:

I used this quick write on the first day of school, and I was touched by my students' responses. They were so hopeful and optimistic! We revisited our writing at the end of the first quarter, and many students rewrote or revised their pieces. We also assessed how well we were meeting our goals for the school year. This quick write could also be used in January to usher in the new calendar year.

REFERENCE

Dakos, K. (2003). Introducing a new me. In *Put your eyes up here and other school poems* (p. 6). New York: Simon & Schuster.

What's Your Fortune?
A Fun-Story Starter

Teresa J. Cornett
4th-Grade Teacher,
George Elementary School, Springdale, Arkansas

Directions:

The teacher should begin by showing a fortune cookie and "thinking out loud" or acting as if he or she has just received the cookie at the end of a meal at a Chinese restaurant. The speaker should note that even though he or she doesn't put much faith in these "fortunes," he or she is surprised at the anticipation he or she feels every time he or she cracks one of these cookies open. (You can embellish this as much as you would like, setting up a restaurant scene, prerecording your voice to play on a tape recorder to make it appear more like they are hearing your thoughts, etc.) Contingent upon your student population, you may want to give each student a real fortune cookie, especially if perhaps they've never seen one.

Next say: *What would I really love to see inside my fortune cookie? What am I getting so hopeful about?*

Distribute strips of 1 × 4-inch paper. Tell the students you're giving them a blank "fortune," and you want them to write down what they would want to see on their fortune.

After they have done the above, I say: *I want you to write about the fortune you've just created. You should write as if the fortune is unfolding before your very eyes. Tell us what happens, how you feel, and how others react.*

After 5 minutes or so, the students should be provided an opportunity to share some of their writings.

Reflection:

I thought of this activity as I walked through my living room one day and noticed a silver fortune cookie I received at a party last summer. Since participating in the Northwest Arkansas Writing Project's Invitational Summer Institute I've discovered that while I'm not in a state of "constant composition," as one writing expert put it, I am in a state of constant idea-gathering for the purpose of increasing writing opportunities in my classroom.

This is a fast and fun opportunity to provide young writers with a story-starter. My students really enjoyed this quick write and appreciated the spark it gave them for creating an interesting little story.

Celebrations: "You're in Charge!"

Cheri Olmstead
4th-Grade Teacher,
Holcomb Elementary, Fayetteville, Arkansas

Directions:

This quick write introduces the theme of "new beginnings" with a personal reflection on the worldwide custom of celebrating an outgoing/incoming year with fireworks and fanfare. Initially, teachers need to discuss and compare the idealized "party scenario" to the more realistic picture of how most people bring in the New Year. Then introduce the picture book, *I'm in Charge of Celebrations* by Byrd Baylor. This is the story of a wise young Native American girl who has her own idea of what a celebration, or a new beginning, should be. Read the story, or a portion of the story, aloud. Ask the students to reflect on special sights, sounds, and moments from the past or visions and hopes for the future.

Then say: *This year you are in charge of your own celebrations. You don't need to wait until mid-December. Plan your first celebration today! Give it a name; think about who, if anyone, should be invited; describe your event. Will it last a moment, an hour, a day, or a month? Where will it take place, or does the place really matter?*

Allow 8–10 minutes to write. Share.

Reflection:

This quick write was inspired by my love of Byrd Baylor's poetic, yet simple appreciation for the beauty in everyday life. I first used it during a staff development workshop at Lingle Middle School in Rogers, Arkansas. The date was January 3, 2000, and Y2K had not come to pass. The vast preparation for a new millennium had loomed before us for many months and was still on our minds. Somehow, this simple book and its message served to remind us of where we were and what we, as individuals, might truly want to celebrate in a new year. Teachers wrote and shared—and became a community of writers.

REFERENCE

Baylor, B. (1986). *I'm in charge of celebrations.* New York: Aladdin.

Salt in His Shoes:
Michael Jordan in Pursuit of a Dream

Mary Wince
Coordinator of Gifted Education,
Valley Springs School, Valley Springs, Arkansas

Directions:

Have you ever wondered what Michael Jordan was like as a kid—before he became a superstar? We get an inside view into Michael's childhood in the book, Salt in His Shoes: Michael Jordan in Pursuit of a Dream. *It was written by Michael's mother, Deloris Jordan, with help from Michael's sister, Roslyn.*

Read the book and then offer the following prompts:

In the book, Michael never gives up on his dream to become a basketball player. Write about your *dream. What will you have to do to achieve your dream? What lesson can you learn from Michael about pursuing your dream?*

During the story, Michael is forced to face a bully, Mark, on the basketball court. Write an experience you've had with a bully.

Michael receives encouragement from his parents and older brothers. Write about a time you received help from those who care about you.

Reflection:
This book about a living sports hero grabs the attention of the audience. Although most young people today are familiar with Michael Jordan, many are unaware of the struggles Michael encountered in pursuing his dream. Try this quick write with students in grades 4–8.

REFERENCE

Jordan, D., & Jordan, R. (2000). *Salt in his shoes: Michael Jordan in pursuit of a dream.* New York: Scholastic.

One Hit Wonder

Chris Goering
Assistant Professor of Curriculum and Instruction,
English Education/Literacy,
University of Arkansas, Fayetteville

Directions:
Present students with examples of several significant life events listed on the board: births, deaths, weddings, divorces, broken bones, romantic relationships, moving, et cetera. Ask them to think back about their life and choose one such event to focus on in this brief writing assignment. As students generate ideas, it is especially helpful if the teacher/leader will share a couple of his/her own life events. Once every member has selected an event, ask the students to choose a song that they either remember as a part of that event or something that connects to it. Again, offering several examples is helpful. *When my stepfather died, they played Eric Clapton's "Tears in Heaven" at his funeral and that song still takes me back to that event when it is played on the radio.* Once the students have selected a song to accompany their event, ask them to explain the life event and the connection to the song as one interwoven paragraph.

Once the students have finished the writing, ask several to share with the whole group or ask them to share in smaller groups. Getting an opportunity to discuss music that they have chosen as important in relation to a significant life event provides students with an interesting twist to personal narrative writing.

Reflection:

Music is a living, breathing, vital component of the lives of today's adolescents; rarely does one see a teenager without music, and when teachers bring it into the classroom, it provides a natural cultural connection to the students' lives and a motivator for students often difficult to reach. While the "One Hit Wonder" assignment is brief, it could be used to start a larger unit on personal narrative writing. One such example is the "Soundtrack of Your Life" (Goering, 2004) assignment where students choose several life events and accompanying music. Ultimately, our successes as teachers rely, at least in part, in how well we know our students' skills, abilities, and interests. Beginning the school year with this assignment provides a glimpse into the lives of our students and helps build bridges of understanding between teacher and student.

REFERENCES

Clapton, E. (1992). Tears in heaven. *Unplugged.* Music Television Networks.

Goering, C. (2004). Music and the personal narrative: The dual track to meaningful writing. *The Quarterly, 26,* 4.

Avocations

M. Darlene Montgomery
10th-, 11th-, & 12th-Grade English Teacher
Northside High School, Fort Smith, Arkansas

Directions:

Write or display a succinct definition of Avocation versus Vocation: avocation—a sideline, a hobby; vocation—a job, work. Bring in or display examples of your favorite activity or hobby (e.g., a story you've written, a poster, an album/DVD cover, a program from a play, a painting, something you've made). You might also have items in your room that demonstrate a strong interest or hobby of yours.

Say: *Students, in order for us to better relate to each other, we're going to focus on avocations. Now an avocation is not necessarily your vocation in life; however, if your job is something you absolutely love to do, it can be both.* (Don't say the following unless true) *For example, one of my avocations is truly also my vocation: I love literature, writing, and working with young adults, so I became your English teacher.* But in case you don't wish to accept that, here are some examples of my other avocations. At home I love to ... (garden—show plant, read scifi—show favorite book, etc.).

Now think of some of your favorite activities (avocations). Quickly list at least five things you love to do. (For seniors I add on "that are not something I would consider illegal or immoral." They chuckle.)

Look over your list and choose one activity you most enjoy. You have 5 minutes to write about that activity.

(Wait a timed 5 minutes) Say: *Time's up. Would anyone like to share his or her writing with the class?*

Reflection:

I use this quick write at the beginning of the year for several reasons: I'm trying to make a connection with my students, so I try to find common ground and interests with them. When I am searching to give them real world explanations or examples later in class, I draw upon these or ask them to discuss an item using their avocation as a point of reference. I also use them when discussing goals and future careers—and the reason to get their education. The definitions are vocabulary builders for the ACT and end of course exams. I try to not only introduce new words frequently, but to get students using them as rapidly as possible.

It's also been my experience that students tend to write better when they are trying to communicate something they are truly interested in and do outside of school. Most students are eager to talk about their activities; however, occasionally you'll have one refuse: "I don't do anything but sleep, work, and come to school." Then I say, "Ok, you can approach this exercise one of two ways. You may discuss something you would like to know how to do, or you may lie and exaggerate to your heart's delight." Lying with permission has a draw all its own for the rebellious. They'll try to either shock or impress you, but at least they'll write. I'm then able to assess student writing ability and creativity as a starting point for that particular class. Students are also asked to save quick writes in their portfolios for future writing opportunities and embellishment. Seniors sometimes refer to them when writing the dreaded college essay.

What Were You Afraid Of?

Jamie Highfill
8th- & 9th- Grade English Teacher,
Woodland Junior High School, Fayetteville, Arkansas

Directions:

Read *No Such Thing* by Jackie French Koller. Say: *Have you ever feared something under the bed and/or experienced any other childhood fears? List some of your childhood fears.*

After the students have written their lists, ask them to develop one of the items on their lists and write for five minutes about that fear. Let them share if they wish.

Reflection:

I used this quick write as a lead in to a discussion of abstract versus concrete ideas, and then moved on to a discussion of how we use symbols to represent those abstract ideas in writing. This also worked well in teaching them the concept of "show, not tell" and concision. The students were given a worksheet in which they were asked to represent fear with a color, a sound, a musical instrument, a taste or food, an animal, a body of water, and a piece of furniture. The students were then asked to take each symbol they chose to represent fear from the list, and make it more specific. The challenge was to do so without using adjectives. I modeled by giving them disgusting/funny examples such as "vomit" instead of "sour" for taste, and an "operating table" instead of just a "table" for a piece of furniture. My students always love it when they get a chance to be gross and disgusting for credit, and some of their ideas were wonderful. One student chose "ocean" for his body of water, but was having a hard time making that more specific, until I asked him what kind of ocean. When he told me a deep, dark, bottomless ocean, I guided him toward the thesaurus, and he chose "abyss."

REFERENCE

Koller, J. (1997) *No such thing*. New York: Scholastic.

Face Your Fears

Norma Prentiss
Literacy Coach,
Nelson-Wilks-Herron Elementary, Mountain Home, Arkansas

Directions:

Say: *We all know what it feels like to be afraid of the unknown. I remember times as a child when I was afraid (e.g., the first day of school, the first time spending the night away from home, the first time I walked home by myself).*

I have a vivid memory of a scary experience. We had just built an addition onto our small house. It was in the back of the house, away from the other bedrooms. I had always shared a room with my three brothers. Now I would have a room all to myself. As a 7-year old, part of me was excited, but another part of me was a little scared. Looking back on that experience as an adult, I see what a big part my imagination played in my fear. Even though the whole event happened in a few minutes, in my mind it felt like an hour! Listen to my story.

Night Fright

One hot, humid, summer night, I lay in my bed in my new room---wide awake. I felt an unnamed evil creep in through my open window. Even the familiar sounds of chirping insects and prowling nocturnal creatures seemed sinister. The moon looked like a silver ball tangled in our big ash tree in the back yard. As the hot wind blew, the branches swayed in the breeze. Moon shadows danced on my bedroom walls. Giant hairy spiders and ghostly ghouls floated around my room. I even imagined that one of them slithered under my bed—waiting for the chance to grab my leg and drag me under the bed to eat me. Hundreds of evil eyes stared wickedly at me from behind my curtains. I shivered in fear as I pulled the sheet over my head. My heart pounded in my chest like a hammer. A cold chill ran down my spine. "Help!" I screamed inside my head. I was paralyzed with fear! Suddenly I couldn't take it anymore. I threw the sheets off and shot out of bed like a rocket. I didn't stop running until I was in my parents' bed, safe and warm.

After that night, Mom and Dad got me a night light. There were no more night frights from that night on!

Say: *Think about a time when you were little. Do you remember a time when something frightened you? Maybe it was an animal or an insect. Maybe it was a person, real or imaginary. It might have been a storm. Write about that moment. Use sensory details to describe to your audience how you felt.*

Give students about 10 minutes and then let them share their stories.

Reflection:
Kids of all ages love scary stories. Because they love being scared, students have been delighted with this activity. It fits in really well around Halloween. I usually dim the lights to set the mood. This activity gives the writer an opportunity to incorporate descriptive words that set the mood.

Truer Words Have Never Been Spoken

Samuel Totten
Founder and Director of the Northwest Arkansas Writing Project and Professor of Curriculum and Instruction, University of Arkansas, Fayetteville

Directions:
First, share the following with your students: *As you know, there are all sorts of famous sayings, adages, and admonitions. Among such are the following:*

- *A stitch in time saves nine;*
- *A penny saved is a penny earned;*
- *The early bird catches the worm;*
- *Neither a lender nor a borrower be;*
- *Haste makes waste;*
- *Don't count your chickens before they hatch;*
- *A coward dies a thousand deaths;*
- *If you can't stand the heat, then get out of the kitchen;*
- *No pain, no gain;*
- *Beggars can't be choosers;*
- *Those who hold the gold, rule;*
- *Beauty is in the eye of the beholder;*
- *A hungry man is an angry man;*
- *A society grows great when men plant trees whose shade they know they shall never sit in;*
- *A tree falls the way it leans;*
- *One in the hand is worth two in the bush; and*
- *He who hesitates is lost.*

Next, Provide This Set of Directions:

Either take one of the aforementioned examples and relate how it applies to your own life by using concrete examples to provide the reader with a solid sense as to how and why that is true. Or, take another well known saying, adage or admonition and use that to show how it is applicable to your own life—again, using concrete examples from your own life to prove your point(s).

Reflection:

This quick write often results in extremely interesting insights by students into phrases they've often heard over and over again but have given little real thought to as they go about their daily lives.

This activity can be tied to an examination of a whole host of literary characters and the lives they lead/led:

- "No pain, no gain" —Huckleberry Finn in Twain's *The Adventures of Huckleberry Finn*
- "A hungry man is an angry man" —Tom Joad in Steinbeck's *Grapes of Wrath*
- "A society grows great when men plant trees whose shade they know they shall never sit in" —Robert Jordan in *For Whom the Bells Toll*
- A tree falls the way it leans —Jay Gatsby in Fitzgerald's *The Great Gatsby*

Sweet Dreams

Mike Thomas
9th-Grade Drama Teacher,
Ramay Junior High, Fayetteville, Arkansas

Say: *I had this crazy dream last night that bears were chasing me through this dark woods and just as one bear starts to attack me I fight him off with a punch in his nose and I keep running then all of a sudden I became a bear and was running with the bears that were chasing me then I stopped and I stood up on my bear hind legs and said in growling bear talk "Hey, who ate my porridge?"*

Explain to students how strange dreams can be. Sometimes they're scary, sometimes pleasant, always a little mysterious, and sometimes revealing. Ask them: What is Astral Projection? Share types of dreams with them: Flying, being chased, reoccurring, déjà vu. Tell them: We dream of people who have passed away. Some say we face our fears in our dreams.

Famous Dreams: Abraham Lincoln dreamed of being shot. Martin Luther King had a dream, Sigmund Freud put a lot of stock in dreams. Artists, writers, musicians draw inspiration from dreams. Read from "Dream Article" in *Life* magazine and Zolar's dream interpretation book. Give everyone a page from the Zolar book to study. *Zolar's Encyclopedia Of Dreams* or any dream interpretation book will do, there are many out there. There are also quite a few websites also to spark a young writer's imagination.

Say: *Now I want you to write about your most vivid or re-occurring or scary dream. A dream you feel comfortable writing about. Take about ten minutes and recall the most you can from a dream and what you think it meant. Be sure to include details, feeling, causes.*

Share dreams and encourage students to keep a dream journal.

Reflection:

I always get some fascinating dream stories from their quick writes. Some students tell me they don't dream or they can't remember upon wakening. In that case, I ask them to write about what they would like to dream about if they could just escape their mind and do and be anything anywhere. Students love to try to find meaning in dreams they have had.

REFERENCE

Zolar. (2004). *Zolar's encyclopedia and dictionary of dreams*. New York: Simon and Schuster.

The Choice of Your Life

Samuel Totten
Founder and Director of the Northwest Arkansas Writing Project, and Professor of Curriculum and Instruction, University of Arkansas, Fayetteville

---

Directions:

The teacher should read the following statement (or a facsimile) to his/ her students. (Note: Teachers may wish to alter/replace the names of certain individuals noted below with the names of those that their students may be more conversant with. In doing so, a teacher should make an effort to include individuals who have vastly different sets of aspirations):

Different people, obviously, have vastly different hopes in regard to what they will do with their lives. Carl Sagan, the famous astronomer, wanted to know everything he possibly could about the universe; Mother Teresa dedicated her life to helping the poorest of the poor in both Calcutta and other places across the globe; Michael Jordan aspired to be the best basketball player who ever played; Nelson Mandela ardently desired to help free his people, black South Africans, from the shackles of Apartheid; and as for Donald Trump, he not only desires great riches and fame but a legacy of having built some of the most famous and beautiful buildings ever built in the United States.

In thinking about living out your own life, what do you hope to accomplish by the time it is over? Is it great wealth? Being famous? Making a great discovery? Being a wonderful, caring parent? Inventing something radically new? Contributing to the betterment of society? Being the most outstanding teacher you possibly could be? Truly being, in the best sense of the word, your brother's or sister's keeper?

Please take 5 to 8 minutes and write about what you hope to accomplish by the end of your life. That is, what do you hope your legacy will be, and why?

Reflection:

This quick write is designed to prod students to really think about what their goals are in life and to, hopefully, begin to consider the value of what they aspire to in life. It's that simple and that profound. This is an excellent quick write to use in a literature class during the study of various characters (e.g., Jay Gatsby or Jordan in *The Great Gatsby*, Robert Jordan in *For Whom the Bell Tolls*, Santiago in *The Old Man and the Sea*, Tom Joad or Rose of Sharon in *Grapes of Wrath*, Bigger Thomas in *Native Son*).

It is also an outstanding quick write to use in a social studies or science class as the class begins the study of a famous person in history.

WRITER'S CRAFT

Hats Off to You

Jackie Hassel
8th-Grade English Teacher,
Ramay Junior High School, Fayetteville, Arkansas

Directions:

Hand out 3 × 5 cards. Then ask the students to: *write down all the times and purposes you've worn a hat or some type of headgear. Go way back in your memory and write what these were. Just list them. There is no need to describe them.*

OK, now pick ONE example from your list and consider the following questions: What did it look like? Why did you wear it? How did the hat make you feel? Did you change in any way?

Let the students share their thoughts about their hats.

Now choose one of the hats that I have brought to class today and examine it very carefully.

After everyone has picked up a hat, ask the students to consider the following questions: *Who would wear it? Why? What would be the occasion or reason? Now imagine that someone you see will now wear this hat by choice.*

Spark the Brain, Ignite the Pen: Quick Writes for Use in Kindergarten Through High School and Beyond, 2nd Edition, pp. 75–129

Bring this person to life on your paper. Describe the person who would wear this particular hat. Consider LOOKS, PERSONALITY, ACTION, VOICE.

Ask for volunteers to share their descriptions.

Reflection:

I find this activity helpful to guide students as they begin to develop characters of a story. Also, they are challenged to think of vivid descriptions that "fit" a particular hat/headgear.

Other possibilities for this activity are the following:

- Could be used in characterizing historical figures.
- Could be used to brainstorm vivid verbs—determine how a person wearing this hat would walk down the street.
- Could use *Aunt Flossie's Hats (and Crabcakes Later)* by Elizabeth Fitzgerald Howard to introduce the hats exercise.
- Students could bring a favorite hat to share something about orally and then write about the hat.
- Students could use this in a geography study and write about hats from different parts of the world.
- Use to generate ideas about headgear worn in various professions/jobs and why.
- In writing descriptions of the wearer, go beyond the obvious and include such detail as the angle of the hat worn; what does this say about the wearer?

REFERENCE

Howard, E. F. (2001). *Aunt Flossie's hats (and crabcakes later)*. New York: Clarion Books.

"... And Another Thing"

Mike Thomas
9th-Grade Drama Teacher
Ramay Junior High, Fayetteville, Arkansas

Directions:

Say: *Have you ever thought of that great comeback on the way home? Quick responses to rude behavior take practice. Today I am going to share a passionate, persuasive letter written by a customer of a certain airline. The letter was written in the heat of the moment. As I read this I want you to think of a time when you wish you would have written a letter to a company or to the editor of a paper.*

Some examples include a pushy store clerk, an ex-whatever, an insensitive boss, a rude waiter, an overzealous policeman, an insult unanswered. This response could begin with the statement, "Oh yeah, well let me tell you something that really bothers me ..." We all suffer little injustices done to us from time to time. This is your calm moment to think back and write what you wished you'd have said as the perfect response.

Before reading ask students to listen for the use of the five senses and voice in the letter. Read the airline letter and ask: Have you ever felt like this guy? Write. Share.

Dear Continental Airlines,

I am disgusted as I write this note to you about the miserable experience I am having sitting in seat 29E on one of your aircrafts. As you may know, this seat is situated directly across from the lavatory, so close that I can reach out my left arm and touch the door. All my senses are being tortured simultaneously. It's difficult to say what the worst part about sitting in 29E really is. Is it the stench of the sanitation fluid that is blown all over my body every 60 seconds when the door opens? Is it the whoosh of the constant flushing? Or is it the passengers' rumps that seem to fit into my personal space like a pornographic jig-saw puzzle?

I constructed a stink-shield by shoving one end of a blanket into the overhead compartment. While effective in blocking at least some of the smell, and offering a small bit of privacy, the rump-on-my-body factor has increased, as without my evil glare passengers feel free to lean up against what they think is some kind of blanketed wall. The next rump that touches my shoulder will be the last!

I am picturing a board room full of executives giving props to the young promising engineer who figured out how to squeeze an additional row of seats onto this plane by putting them next to the lavatory.

I would like to flush his head in the toilet that I am close enough to touch, and taste, from my seat. Putting a seat here was a very bad idea. I just heard a man groan in there! Ugh!

Worse yet, is I've paid over $400 for the honor of sitting in this seat! Does your company give refunds? I'd like to go back where I came from and start over. Seat 29E could only be worse if it was located inside the bathroom.

I wonder if my clothing will retain the sanitizing odor … what about my hair! I feel like I'm bathing in a toilet bowl of blue liquid. I am filled with a deep hatred for your plane designer and a general dis-ease that may last for hours.

We are finally descending, and soon I will be able to tear down the stink-shield, but the source will remain.

I suggest that you initiate immediate removal of this seat from all of your crafts. Just remove it, and leave the smoldering brown hole empty, a place for sturdy/non-absorbing luggage maybe, but not human cargo.

Customer in seat 29E.

Reflection:

Ninth graders jump on this. A majority already see their lives as very unfair, so this assignment gives them permission to complain about it. They write to exboyfriends/girlfriends, parents, first time bosses, authority figures, and video game companies. The letter is a good way to start the lesson with a laugh. Their writing is often funny.

Reading With Your "Author Glasses" On or "Hey! I Could Do That!"

Clare Lesieur
K-4 Academic Coach,
Harrison School District, Harrison, Arkansas

Directions:

As a way to focus students on author's craft, my students and I read like authors. Anytime I conduct a read-aloud, the kids are asked to listen for the purpose of sharing great techniques that they could use in their own writing. Often, we connect the day's writing mini-lesson to the reading. For example, "Let's listen to how the author builds up to the good part," or "Pay attention to the way the author ends this story," or "After we read this story, let's discuss parts of the story that really stick in your mind. How did the author make that happen?"

With some practice, the students will begin to identify craft elements themselves. We conclude a reading with a round of applause for the author and then have share time for comments about craft. Students will say things such as, "I like the way the author described the clouds as wispy and billowy. I could almost picture myself laying in the grass and looking up at the sky," or "The author started the story with a question. That was a good way to hook the reader," or "The word ____ really stuck in my head. I would like to use that word in my writing."

This think-aloud activity can evolve into a quick write. After reading a story whole-class (or even in response to independent reading), ask students to write a few ideas from the story that they could apply to their own writing. The focus here is on craft. Allow share time, and encourage kids to try some of these techniques in their own pieces.

Reflection:

Once we begin to think of ourselves as writers, we cannot help but read with our "author glasses" on. Authors learn from each other, so why not invite some of the greatest writing teachers into your classroom by reading a variety of writing with your students? I read aloud to my fourth graders every day, and we note elements of craft in our reflections about the stories. During writer's workshop, students will often point out a craft element in their own writing and credit another author for inspiring that technique.

I Wanna: Persuasive Writing

Betty Pittman
K-6 Library Media Specialist,
Hackett Elementary School, Hackett, Arkansas

Directions:

This is a fun way to introduce persuasive writing to students. After reviewing the term "persuasive" with students, read aloud *I Wanna Iguana* by Karen Kaufman Orloff, a story of a little boy who engages in a letter writing campaign with his mother to try to convince her to let him get an iguana as a pet.

After the story has been read, ask the students to sit quietly for a few moments to think of something they have wanted very badly but have been refused. It can be a pet, but it does not have to be. Now ask them to write, in friendly-letter form, a letter to convince someone that they should have what it is they want. They can be creative in their reasoning, but they need to present convincing arguments.

Reflection:
   I Wanna Iguana is a good selection to introduce students to persuasive writing in a way that is fun but effective. Most students, especially elementary students, want a pet at some time, so they can identify with the story. High school students could also relate it to their desire for a car or a cell phone. This quick write could also be used to reinforce the mechanics of writing a friendly letter for younger students.

REFERENCE

Orloff, K. (2004). *I wanna iguana*. New York: Putnam.

Things Aren't Always What They Seem

Jeanne King
*6th- & 7th-Grade Gifted and Talented Enrichment,
Holt Middle School and Owl Creek School,
Fayetteville, Arkansas*

Directions:
   The purposes of this quick write are to encourage risk taking, to create openness to what poetry can be, to write within an accepting environment, and to encourage a sense of playfulness.
   The materials needed are cards made from unrecognizable photographs. These are the type of photos found in many puzzle books or science magazines for children, where a close-up or detail of an object makes it hard to know just what the object really is. The photographs can be randomly chosen or could relate to a subject being taught. They may be found ready-made, or they may be created by cutting up large photographs into smaller sections.

Say: *Each of you has a card with a photograph on it. Now, you may or may not be able to tell what that photo is. But it doesn't really matter. In fact, I want you NOT to worry about what it is!*

I'm going to help you to collect your thoughts about your photo. You will find as we go along that some of your ideas will overlap into different categories, and that's okay. Just follow along and get your ideas on paper.

First, I'd like you to focus on the lines you see in your photo. Write down words or phrases that come to you when you look at the lines. Pause to allow students to look, think, and write after each set of directions.

Now, look at the colors. Give them the most descriptive names you can. For instance, blue may become turquoise or midnight blue.

What shapes do you see? Think organic as well as geometric. You may even have to make up a name for your shapes.

Now, I would think that when you look at your photo, you get an impression or a feeling from that picture. Use words to capture the emotion of your photo.

Look back over the lists you have made and add anything to them that you would like to at this time.

One of the things we know about writing is that sometimes it's a risk. You may be asked to write in a way that is unfamiliar to you or to use words that seem strange. But we also know that in a writing community, our writing is accepted and that the only way to grow is to try new things. So here is something new for you to try. Using the colorful, strong language you have collected, write a short poem. You can add words, combine words, change words. You can put the words in a new order, and you don't have to use all of your words. Take what you have on your paper and create a poetic piece of writing!

Give the opportunity to share photographs and poems after students have written.

Samples:

It is evident that the poems have nothing to do with what the photographs actually depict.

From a photo of an elephant's skin
From far above
I see the roads of my life
Criss-crossing, rambling, etched
Heading to a destiny
I have yet to discover.
Like a puzzle unfinished
Paths will come together
To lead me to the unknown.

From a photo of the underside of an umbrella
Behind the shade a spider lies

I watch it closely with my eyes.
The tears stream down as it crawls about
I am so afraid I stifle a shout.
I pick up a book and slowly walk near.
I think, "I can't wait to splat you, my dear."
I hit the spider, the guts squirt about.
I finally let out that stifled shout.
The red and pink against the shade
Oh dear, poor spider, what a mess I made.

Reflection:

This is a nonthreatening way to ease into poetry writing. The resulting poems are often short, which is manageable to students, and since no particular form is required, it provides an insight as to the level of sophistication students bring to the study of poetry.

I've Got the Blues

Lynette Terrell
7th-Grade English Teacher,
J.O. Kelly Middle School, Springdale, Arkansas

Directions:

When my students enter the room they hear B.B. King singing *Everyday (I Have the Blues)*. I often get some initial groans, "Is this old people's music, Miss?" Soon they're swaying and tapping along. After the song I ask them if they've ever had the blues. Of course they have! Why? Because they've had to move, their boyfriend/girlfriend broke up with them, or maybe it was because they flunked a test. We all get the blues because we all encounter problems in our lives. How do we deal with these problems? We can talk to someone. We can write a letter or in a diary. Langston Hughes wrote poetry about his blues, and he wrote many poems in the same form as a blues song: one long line repeated followed by a shorter line that adds a little upbeat feeling. Why the change? Even though problems are a fact of life and we all get the blues and feel down, no one wants to stay that way! I play the tape that lets Langston Hughes tell about his blues poetry. I write his example on the board. Then I ask my students what problems are called in literature. I get the correct answer, conflicts. I ask what conflicts Billie Jo, Ma, Daddy, and Mad Dog faced. These are characters in *Out of the Dust,* the book we just finished reading. We discuss the conflicts, and then I instruct the students to write a blues poem in the voice of one of these characters.

Reflection:

This exercise could be adapted for any grade with any character. Junie B., Wilbur, Harry, and Rose of Sharon all had the blues. It can also be used for a journal entry for students to write about their own blues.

REFERENCES

King, B. B. (1994.). *Blues on top of blues* [CD]. CEMA Special Markets.
Huges, L. (1980 & 1992). *Langston Hughes reads.* New York: HarperCollins.

Poems for Two Voices

Lynette Terrell
7th-Grade English Teacher,
J.O. Kelly Middle School, Springdale, Arkansas

Directions:

As an English teacher, it's my job to teach my students to write. This means I encourage creative and expressive writing, but I also teach practical writing. Therefore, I incorporate strategies for them to experience writing across the curriculum. One good way to do this is by using Paul Fleischman's *Joyful Noise Poems for Two Voices.* I read two poems ("Book Lice" and "The Digger Wasp") and we talk about them. We discuss how they teach about the particular insect in a poetic way. We talk about the style and how the poems are indeed written for two voices. Then I tell them they're going to write a poem with a partner in the same style, and one that teaches. I ask what they're studying in science. I list what they tell me on the board. I then do the same thing for math, geography, health, art, etc. After we've made the lists for each subject, I then pick a particular area in the subject and ask what specifically could be taught. We list ideas for narrowing the focus. Then, I let them create.

Samples by Students:

Numbers *Easy equations*	*Numbers*
	Adding, subtracting
Hard equations	
	Multiplying, dividing
Numbers *Pi*	*Numbers*
	3.14
Algebra	
	Calculus
Geometry	
	Measurement
Problem	
	Solving
Numbers *Fractions*	*Numbers*
	Decimals
Percentages *40 people get on your bus*	*Percentages*
	25 get off
36 get back on	
	They pass by the same house twice
10 more people get off *What color is the bus driver's eyes?*	*What color is the bus driver's eyes?*

—Lauren and Michelle

Bacteria have *Three basic shapes*	
	Do you know what they are?
They are	
	Rod like, spherical like *Spiral like*
Spiral like *They can be found on your skin*	
	Even in your intestine
Are bacteria good or bad?	
	They can be both. *Some fight diseases* *And some cause diseases*
Some fight diseases	
Are they heterotroph or autotroph?	
	They are both
They obtain their own food, and *They make their own food.* *Bacteria are found in most of the food we eat*	*They make their own food.*
	Like cheese

And sourdough bread
Bacteria
Are a part of life

        And sourdough bread
        Bacteria
        Are a part of life

—Danika and Jordan

Reflection:

This is an excellent writing-to-learn exercise. My students have written poems for two voices using what they've learned from all subject areas—even their vocabulary lessons in English class. It's also a great exercise for English Language Learners. Beginning ELL's can simply say the lines in unison. Intermediate learners can speak individual parts but have the comfort of a partner in writing and performing. Advanced learners can add some of their first language to the mix!

REFERENCE

Fleischman, P. (1988). *Joyful noise poems for two voices*. New York: Scholastic

Word Poems and the Content Areas

Rita S. Caver
10th-Grade Advanced Placement United States History Teacher
Fayetteville High School, Fayetteville, Arkansas

Directions:

In this activity, we will take a word group (usually a set of 4 words) and put them together in a way that makes sense to create a feeling or an image.

Say: *Look at these words: courage lion butterflies father*

Can you see a way that they can go together? Is there a certain image or feeling that comes to mind when you read any or all of these words? Now we'll write a poem together. Here are the rules:

1. You may change the form of the word (suffixes, prefixes, plural to singular, etc.)
2. You may add as many additional words as you need.

3. You may have as many lines as you need, but you must have at least three.
4. Do not try to force a rhyme.

We will work as a group on the first one. Write lines on the board, play with them, and try to put them together into a coherent poem.

Samples of Student Work:

Like a lion,
my father dozes on the porch,
I was in my room
when he came home.
Has he seen the broken window?
Has my mother told him yet?
My stomach's full of butterflies.
Courage, a lion's courage—
do I have it?

My father
is the lion of my family.
From him, I gain courage
when the butterflies
batter against the
sides of my stomach.

Reflection:

Word poems are one of my favorite writing activities because the students will regularly write something brilliant in just a few minutes. Even students who don't normally share their work will often share their poems. Students who are not the stars of the class will regularly shine in this activity. These will work with any subject area. In addition, students can use these quick poems to work on editing their work. These poems lend themselves to that process. Thanks to Lynette Terrell, a teacher consultant with the Northwest Arkansas Writing Project, for sharing this idea. Parts of this lesson originally came from an Arts With Education Institute at the Walton Arts Center in Fayetteville, Arkansas and presented by Sandy Lynne.

CoCo's Voice

Judy L. Davis
2nd-Grade Teacher,
Deer Consolidated Schools, Deer, Arkansas

Directions:

Missing: One Stuffed Rabbit is a story about a classroom's stuffed rabbit. The rabbit goes home with a different student each night. Each student writes in the rabbit's diary, pretending to be the rabbit and recording what they do together. The rabbit gets lost and is later recovered.

Read the story to the class. Then present the class with a stuffed animal and have them pretend to be that animal. They are to write from the point of view of the stuffed animal, describing what the stuffed animal will do with them at home. Give the students about 5 minutes to respond. Ask for volunteers to share their writing.

Reflection:

This was one of my class's favorite activities. After the quick write, the students were each allowed to take CoCo, my stuffed monkey, home and write about the activities they shared as if he or she were CoCo. Over the years I've found that the families become very involved with CoCo. As one might imagine, CoCo has also become a very "lively" and "alive" member of our class. In fact, one summer I had to seek special permission from the class to keep him so I could introduce him to my National Writing Project fellows.

I believe that such an activity with a stuffed animal would work well with grades K–4. I've often pondered over whether one couldn't use an object such as a tennis ball, glove, or live animal to get older students involved.

This has proven to be an easy way for me to introduce "point of view" to my students.

Materials:

Stuffed animal, paper, pencil, notebook for journal, backpack, and *Missing: One Stuffed Rabbit* by Maryann Cocca-Leffler.

REFERENCE

Cocca-Leffler, M. (1994). *Missing: One stuffed rabbit*. New York: Scott Foresman.

Have I Got a Story for You!

Priscilla Kumpe
8th- and 9th-Grade Gifted and Talented Teacher,
Ramay Junior High School, Fayetteville, Arkansas

Directions:
For analyzing attributes, students are given a packet of assorted buttons to examine, sort, classify, and identify attributes. As they sort, the teacher should circulate and note the various ways students are classifying the buttons. Encourage students to arrange them in more than one way. Keep at it for about 5 minutes.

Next, ask: *What attributes do all the buttons have in common?* (Some may answer, for example, size, color, function, or age.)

As a group, list (on the board or overhead) all the other attributes that can be used to describe buttons: color, size, number of holes, materials used, degree of ornamentation, shapes, texture, multiple holes versus shank construction.

Taking the concept of attributes further, the teacher could say:

When we talk about a person's or animal's attributes, we often include how they act and feel. Which of your buttons might you describe as powerful? Private? Vain? Mundane? Curious? Adventurous?

- *Which of your buttons would sing the loudest?*
- *Which are female? Male?*
- *Which would be the most independent? The most dependent on others?*
- *Which might enjoy heavy metal music, or classical?*
- *Which would consider itself artistic? Who would its favorite artist be?*
- *If you have any buttons that you consider totally unique, how do you think it feels to be one of a kind instead of part of a group?*
- *If these were high school students, which would be the jocks? The geeks? The socialites? The foreign exchange students?*
- *What other ideas do you have?*
- *Pick one of your buttons. Imagine, now, that you are that button.*
- *You have certain attributes that can be seen and described.*
- *Add to that your feelings about being a button.*
- *What experiences have you had in your button life?*
- *What was it like in the store before someone picked you out to take home?*

- *How did your owners treat you?*
- *What is it like being with all these other buttons in a box?*

Give writing time. Share.

What have we done? Have the students state in their own words what they did and how this was different from other kinds of writing.

Ask what "encounter" means to them. Brainstorm a list on the board. The discussion could include a reference to the movie *Close Encounters of the Third Kind*, in which the character sleeps, eats, and is totally involved with the experience with aliens. *Webster's* definition includes the following: (n) a direct, often momentary meeting; a chance meeting. (v) to come upon face-to-face; to meet by chance.

In an encounter group the members try to develop the capacity to express feelings and to form emotional ties by unrestrained confrontation of individuals.

Identify the type of writing the students have just done as a "Creative Encounter." In doing so, the teacher should delineate the process in which the writer becomes something else and responds as though he or she were the new thing and incorporates these suggested categories:

- *Identity and role of object*
- *Description—using sensory information*
- *Emotions—how you would react if presented with certain situations and how it feels to be this thing*
- *Adaptation—how you change or add to yourself in this new role*
- *Point of View—how you view the world around you*

Reflection:

When I have done this with teachers in the Northwest Arkansas Writing Project workshops and with students, they are immediately engaged and eager to share which of their buttons exhibits certain personality traits and feelings. Because the descriptive aspects of the exercise are apparent, when they select one button and write from its perspective, they are able to work the description into the life story of the button. Often, having already identified a "personality attribute" of the button, the story evolves easily. Writers find that they really are looking at the world from a different perspective. They enjoy adding the whimsical elements, emotions, and details of the button's experiences that relate to its appearance and attributes. I always hear original and engaging stories when the participants share.

Students tell me that this approach makes them think, and that it is fun.

REFERENCE

Speilberg, S. (Director), Philips, J., & Philips, M. (Producers). (1977). *Close encounters of the third kind* [Film]. Columbia Pictures.

The Mysteries of Harris Burdick

Clare Lesieur
4th-Grade Teacher,
Skyline Heights Elementary School, Harrison, Arkansas

Directions:

Ask the students such questions as: *What is a mystery?* Discuss. *What are some ways authors use inferences to lead us astray in a mystery?* Then discuss their answers.

Read the preface to *The Mysteries of Harris Burdick,* and then share the illustrations and accompanying captions that follow. The illustrations were supposedly left by a children's author who mysteriously vanished. These unique pictures really get the creative juices flowing. It is difficult to view them without formulating many story ideas. Discuss some ideas as a group.

Make several copies of each illustration from the book. Let each student choose one illustration to write a mysterious story about. Remind them to experiment using inferences to create intrigue and possibly mislead the reader. As a challenge, see if students can incorporate the illustration's caption into the story.

Allow time to share. To set the mood and for extra fun, dim the lights!

Reflection:

This writing activity is an oldie but goodie that works well as a quick write. It is interesting to see how students write such different stories from the same illustrations. My students love to do this activity again and again, using different pictures as prompts. This especially works well as part of an author study on Chris Van Allsburg.

REFERENCE

Van Allsburg, C. (1984). *The mysteries of Harris Burdick*. Boston: Houghton Mifflin.

How Lame!

Samuel Totten
*Founder and Director of the Northwest Arkansas Writing Project,
and Professor of Curriculum and Instruction,
University of Arkansas, Fayetteville*

Directions:

Read the students a short, preferably somewhat humorous, piece that is riddled with clichés. (See example below.) After reading it to them, ask them to share their "gut responses" to it. What did they like? Not like? If they neglect to mention the clichés, then the teacher should broach the issue him- or herself: *Was there anything that struck your ear as odd?* If the students don't jump for that "bait," then ask, *Were there any lines in this piece of writing that you've heard repeatedly anywhere else, and if so, what were they?* That could be followed up with a question along the lines of, *What is your initial response to hearing a piece with so many clichés in it?* If the students are not familiar with the term "clichés," then this is the time to introduce the term and to ask them to define it based on the old, tired phrases they've heard in the piece of writing.

(Optional):

Depending on the age and knowledge base of one's students, one may or may not wish to have the students take part in a brainstorming session in which they list all of the clichés they can think of within 1–2 minutes. These should be listed on the board and left there throughout the quick write.

Next, the students should be asked to write a piece in which he or she uses one cliché after another to describe, for example, "the typical school day." Often it is easier if the students are provided with a topic to write on, one that is easy for every student to address—such as (1) the food in the school cafeteria, (2) mom's cooking, (3) school rules, (4) rules at home, (5) favorite meal, (6) birthday parties, (7) all-time favorite teacher, (8) worst vacation, (9) summer school, or (10) best friends.

Reflection:

The reaction to this quick write has always been extremely favorable. Most students are familiar with clichés, even the youngest—even if they do not know what the word "cliché" means. The pieces that the students generate are generally creative and quite humorous. This is a painless, and enjoyable, way to introduce students to the concept of "clichés" and/

or the rationale behind the need to limit them in one's speech and writing—unless there is an express purpose for using one or more, such as in this quick write.

Sample of Student Response:

"Hellllo!" the guy, tall as a tree said.

"What?" asked his buddy, Red, a short fellow with red hair and freckles.

"How lame!" the tall, lanky guy cried out.

"What?!"

"Duh!"

"What?"

"Your idea! It's so full of holes it'd sink a boat!"

"Says who?"

"Says me. You know what I mean?"

"Like I can read your mind?" his friend asked, getting red as a beet.

"Are you that out of it?" the tall guy asked, leaning his string bean body forward as he got in his friend's face.

As the boys' argument was going nowhere fast, a girl, pretty as a peach, walked by and smiled at them.

"Whoa, check her out!" the redhead said, his eyes spinning like roulette balls. "Did you see her?"

"Am I blind?"

"Yeah, blind as a bat with those big thick goggles you call glasses."

Ignoring the insult as if it was water off a duck's back, his friend shot back: "Sticks and stones will break my bones, but words will never hurt me."

"Yeah, well, if you think she's so cute, then quit sitting there like a bump on a log and go ask her out!"

At the thought, the tall kid's eyes got as big as saucers.

"Ah, you're afraid of your own shadow, aren't you?"

"Takes one to know one."

"You wouldn't talk to her to save your life."

"Look who's talking!"

Come Take a Free Write

Chris Goering
*Assistant Professor of Curriculum and Instruction,
English Education/Literacy,
University of Arkansas, Fayetteville*

Directions:

According to *Writing Down the Bones* by Natalie Goldberg, a timed writing exercise is the "basic unit of writing practice" (p. 8). Teenagers do not like sitting for a timed period and writing, especially when "how" they write is structured. When students hear different genres of music, however, they automatically make different connections and have an abundance of source material and motivation to start writing. Begin this assignment by explaining Goldberg's six principles of free writing.

1. *Keep your hand moving.* (Don't pause to reread the line you have just written. That's stalling and trying to get control of what you're saying.)
2. *Don't cross out.* (That is editing as you write. Even if you write something you didn't mean to write, leave it.)
3. *Don't worry about spelling, punctuation, grammar.* (Don't even care about staying within the margins and lines on the page.)
4. *Lose control.*
5. *Don't think. Don't get logical.*
6. *Go for the jugular* (If something comes up in your writing that is scary or naked, dive right into it. It probably has lots of energy.) (p. 8).

Goldberg suggests that these rules must be followed in order to ensure a clear path to writing. This process takes practice for students because they are programmed to be reserved and overly concerned with formal writing. While this assignment remains valid as it is described, adding the element of background music to it allows discussion of mood and tone within free writing. By switching the music clips at two minute intervals during the assignment from extremes such as Metallica to James Taylor to Beethoven to the Cars, students' writing changes as the music does. As the students choose to connect, or disconnect, to the music being played, discussions of tone and mood are fruitful. Asking the students to share their reactions briefly constitutes an essential part of this assignment.

Reflection:

Using this assignment with students brings a variety of reactions to the music being played. As surely as some students will write along with a metal group such as Metallica, others will completely stop writing. It is effective to have Goldberg's six keys to free writing displayed or projected in the room. The more repetition students have with activities such as this, the more comfortable and receptive they become to an assignment that seems like a break from the educational rigor of the day to day to language arts classroom. With that break comes an opportunity to demonstrate what a successful writer, here Goldberg, does to hone her skills.

REFERENCE

Goldberg, N. (1986). *Writing down the bones: Freeing the writer within*. Boston: Shambhala.

Ridiculous Rhymes

Jane Keith
2nd-Grade Teacher,
Joe Mathias Elementary School, Rogers, Arkansas

Directions:

Say: *Today we are going to take something we know and have fun with it. We will experiment with words. We will toss them around, and make them fit. We are going to mold and shape and have fun as we write parodies of nursery rhymes! First, let's think. Why were nursery rhymes written?* (1) To deal with real life; 2) To deal with childhood fears; (3) To refer to another piece of literature, or poke fun at a written piece or event; (4) For fun—the rhythms are fun to repeat; 5) For political commentary about kings and queens

Read or recite a nursery rhyme. Define parody (a literary or artistic work that broadly mimics an author's characteristic style and holds it up to ridicule). Model a parody of a nursery rhyme. *Say: Write a parody of your favorite nursery rhyme.*

Samples of Student Work:

Parody of "Little Boy Blue"

"Little Pink Goat"
Little pink goat,
Come, sing with me,
Billy's in the barnyard,
And Nanny's up a tree.
Where is the little pink goat
Who won't sing with me?
She's jumped the fence and is with
the pigs three.

Parody of "Hey Diddle Diddle"

"Hey, Robbie, Robbie"
Hey, Robbie, Robbie
The horse had a hobby.
The mole dug a tunnel to the moon.
The little chick quacked
to see such a hole
and said, "Did you dig with a spoon?"

Reflection:

As a child, I loved to play with words. My mother and I would make up poems paraphrasing the rhymes and rhythms of nursery rhymes. I remember jumping rope and hopping, doing just that! When I presented this "fun with words and rhythm" activity to my class of second graders, they responded in like manner. I heard poetry with the cadence of nursery rhymes as they played "hand games" on the playground or jumped rope in simple communication with each other. I heard explosions of laughter and watched as they tried to outdo one another. Words are to be rolled around, experimented with, and just enjoyed. This quick write does that, but in addition, it translates into oral activities and games that further vocabulary and rhyming words.

Love Your Lemon

Denise Nemic
Composition Teacher,
Northwest Arkansas Community College, Bentonville, Arkansas

Directions:

The purpose of this quick write is to exercise our powers of observation and to develop an appreciation for the things that make us unique. To conduct this quick write, you will need to provide a lemon for each participant. Place the lemons in a sack, and pass the sack around to everyone.

Say: *Each person should take one lemon. Each person should carefully observe his or her lemon. IMPORTANT: Do not mark on the lemon! Do not taste the lemon! List all the features of your lemon. Draw your lemon if you wish. Smell it and touch it.*

After several minutes of observation and descriptive writing, all lemons should be placed back into the sack. Shake the sack and then pour out the lemons on a central table. Everyone must find his or her lemon. (Surprise: Everyone is able to do so!!!)

Say: *Think about a special loved one. Make a list (or write in any genre you wish) of the qualities and attributes that make this loved one unique: personality quirks, attitudes, activities, style, enthusiasms, ways of reacting and relating to others and events, and so forth. Write for five to ten minutes.*

Ask the following questions: *How do you know this loved one from any other on the planet? What does this loved one do, how does this loved one act, where and how does this loved one affect your life? What would life be like without your loved one? What would be missing in your life if this loved one weren't in it? What can you do because of this loved one that you wouldn't be able to do otherwise? What does this loved one help you realize or understand about yourself or anything at all? What is a favorite phrase or activity of your loved one?*

Reflection:

This exercise can help writers learn to observe and then articulate the aspects of loved ones that make them the special ones they are. Noticing these attributes and uniqueness can help writers learn to "paint" characters more fully and to create round characters instead of flat ones. It can also help writers learn to see and appreciate the attributes or qualities of other people who still affect and influence their lives.

Hoot's Diner: Place With Personality

Sharla Keen-Mills, NBCT,
8th- & 9th-Grade English Teacher,
Woodland Junior High School, Fayetteville, Arkansas

Directions:

This quick write provides a fun way to practice using sensory details, using description for content development, and creating a setting.

First, share a memory about a dining establishment from your past. In my case, my parents had one of those Blue Plate Special cafes that served breakfast and lunch. The fried chicken was crispy and the biscuits were fluffy. Right down the road was the less reputable version of my parents' cafe: Hoot's. Hoot's was known for fiery chili and greasy fries but not the best hygiene. Wilma, Hoot's waitress, was also quite a character, so I have my students imagine the waitress and Hoot's place when they write this exercise.

Next, distribute copies of the following situation and questions. Reluctant writers often surprise themselves when they've had time to ask preliminary questions before they write. Depending on your students, allow 5 to 10 minutes to answer questions.

Hoot's Diner: Place with Personality

The situation: You're driving through a town far from home when your radiator starts steaming. You manage to find a mechanic at a gas station who can fix your car, but it will take a few hours. You ask the mechanic if there is a place to eat while you wait. He points across the road to Hoot's Diner. Because you have little choice, you head inside and take a seat at the first booth on the left. You're stunned by the filth you see. Take a few minutes and answer the questions below.

Questions:

1. What does the floor look like?
2. Describe the menu.
3. Describe Wilma, the waitress.
4. Is there anything on the walls?
5. What is playing on the jukebox or television?
6. Name six specific smells.

7.   Hoot is cooking behind the counter. What is he like?
8.   Describe Moe, Hoot's dog who is snoring in the corner.
9.   Who is sitting in the next booth? What are they talking about?
10. Wilma brings your food. What is it like?

Once students have answered the questions, distribute index cards or post cards you've made on cardstock. Instruct students to write a postcard to someone at home describing their experience in Hoot's Diner. Remind them that either poetry or prose is appropriate. A postcard-size piece of writing is less intimidating to struggling writers. For a class of experienced and fluent writers, give letter-sized cards so they have more space available if needed. Allow students 5 to 10 minutes to write.

Share student writing as time allows. Sometimes students share with each other in groups, and the group picks one postcard to share with the class.

Reflection:

At the annual meeting of the National Council of Teachers of English in 2006, Mark Larsen and Robert Boone did a workshop about helping students write creatively, called "Moe's Cafe." They demonstrated this technique of setting up a situation and providing questions for prewriting. I recognized that this method would create a safe writing experience for students, so I adapted it for use in my classroom to practice using sensory details, developing plot with description, and creating a setting. However, the technique can be used in any content area to improve student response. For example, in a history class studying Western Expansion and contact with American Indians, students could either be captives or chance visitors in an American Indian camp in a given year. Their descriptions of the sights, sounds, and smells would help the teacher assess the depth of student understanding. The students would also make a personal connection to the learning. My students enjoy this quick write so much that some version of Hoot's Diner often shows up in their creative narratives and poems. I have also adapted using prewriting questions and a short response to studies of literature and genre.

REFERENCE

Larsen, M., & Boone, R. (2006). *Moe's cafe: 48 decidedly different creative writing prompts.* Tucson, AZ: Goodyear Books.

"She Did WHAT?!"

Jamie Highfill
8th- & 9th- Grade English Teacher,
Woodland Junior High School, Fayetteville, Arkansas

Directions:

Show kids the book and then play several audio selections from *Amy's Answering Machine*.

Afterwards, ask the kids why they thought the selections were funny. How would they like their mothers or fathers to leave them messages like that? What about the messages is irritating? Embarrassing? How have their own mothers or fathers done things that irritated or embarrassed them? Share an anecdote of your own.

Then have the kids take about 5 minutes to write about a time that their mother or father or other older relative did something to irritate them or embarrass them in front of someone else.

Finally, say: *I know that there are topics you discuss with your friends that you would NEVER discuss with me, right? Just like Amy's mother, there are some topics I would not want my mother prying into with me either. Amy's mother did not take something vital into account when leaving messages on her daughter's machine, did she? What would that be?*

Knowing when it is appropriate to discuss some topics and with whom means that we have to take our audience into account. Knowing who our audience is will tell us how we should talk to them.

Knowing who our audience is will also determine what topics are okay to discuss as well, right? Would you want to tell your principal about the last time you had a sleepover, particularly, if you did something he/she might raise his/her eyebrows over?

Reflection:

Each year, I've found that teaching students about audience and appropriateness becomes more and more difficult. With the increase in access to technology and instant messaging, students use more and more internet abbreviations in their writing because they use them in their authentic communications with their friends online. This lesson came out of a discussion with a colleague of the audio tracks from *Amy's Answering Machine* that are played with regularity on NPR (National Public Radio). I thought the tracks were hilarious and wondered how I could use them with my own students, and when we started persuasive writing, it hit me. These tracks were perfect for getting the point across about considering one's audience, and making communication appropriate for whomever we would be talking to. The kids LOVED the tracks; however, there are some that would not be appropriate for junior high students.

The stories the kids shared were hilarious, and really did show that the more things change, the more they stay the same. Adolescents STILL hate for their parents to indicate there is any relationship between them, especially in public.

REFERENCE

Borkowsky, A. (2001). *Amy's answering machine*. New York: Pocket Books. (Several tracks are also available on the NPR Web site for free.)

Famous First Pages: A Syntax Study

Shelley Dirst
Literacy Specialist,
Arkansas Department of Education

Directions:

As students become fluent writers, it is important that they intentionally employ syntax to suit a specific purpose. It is a question of style. This quick write is one way to help them explore how an author manipulates syntax from the very first lines of a work in order to achieve a desired effect. Following an analysis of syntax at work and a subsequent quick write, students can then be asked to apply this syntactical awareness to a piece (of any mode) they are currently writing.

Say: *You know that as a writer, you make choices depending on the effect you want to achieve. These choices are elements of style. In addition to the imagery, information, and vocabulary you select, one aspect of style is that of syntax. Syntax refers to the way you structure your sentences, including the length, rhythm, beginnings, voice (active or passive), word order and arrangement of ideas (parallel structure, interrupted sentences, antithesis, periodic sentences), sentence type (declarative, etc) and sentence structure (simple, compound, etc.).To illustrate what is meant by purposeful syntax, I want to share some models from the first pages of famous novels. In these lines, the authors invite the reader into a world and set the mood. Let's read these aloud* (ask for student volunteers).

1. *Commander Victor Henry rode a taxi-cab home from the Navy building on Constitution Avenue, in a gusty gray March rainstorm that matched his mood. (Herman Wouk,* The Winds of War)

2. *What a lark! What a plunge! For so it had always seemed to her, when, with a little squeak of the hinges, which she could hear now, she had burst open the French windows and plunged at Bourton into the open air. (Virginia Woolf,* Mrs. Dalloway)

After these are read, have a general discussion to analyze the syntax of each and the effect created. How does Woolf's differ from Wouk's? You might, for example, discuss Wouk's long, steady, heavily embedded sentence vs. Woolf's staccato phrases amplified by the long, choppy, heavily embedded sentence. Discuss what the syntax conveys about each of the speakers.

You may also want to quote from Maureen Howard's foreword to *Mrs. Dalloway*: "Placed like stones at the rim of a billowing tent, these clear little sentences seem necessary stakes in the shimmering flow of language and emotion that strains, in paragraph after paragraph, to contain the intricacies of life."

Say: *Now that you are thinking in terms of syntax, I have a challenge for you. Listen to some additional lines from the first pages of famous novels:.*

1. *I am Myra Breckinridge whom no man will ever possess. (Gore Vidal,* Myra Breckinridge)

2. *It was the best of times, it was the worst of times, it was the age of wisdom, it was the age of foolishness, it was the epoch of belief, it was the epoch of incredulity, it was the season of Light, it was the season of Darkness, it was the spring of hope, it was the winter of despair, we had everything before us, we had nothing before us, we were all going direct to Heaven, we were all going direct the other way—in short, the period was so far like the present period, that some of its noisiest authorities insisted on its being received, for good or for evil, in the superlative degree of comparison only. (Charles Dickens,* A Tale of Two Cities)

3. *If you really want to hear about it, the first thing you'll probably want to know is where I was born, and what my lousy childhood was like, and how my parents were occupied and all before they had me" (J.D. Salinger,* Catcher in the Rye)

4. *Nobody was really surprised when it happened, not really, not on the subconscious level where savage things grow. (Steven King,* Carrie)

Say: *Select one of the above quotes and analyze the syntax. How is syntax used for effect? What image of the speaker does the syntax (sentence structure) reveal? What can you imagine about the book based on the first line?*

After they have written, ask students to form small groups based on the lines they have chosen so that they can compare responses. Then, allow for whole group discussion and reflection on the writer's craft.

Finally, ask them to emulate the syntactical examples and apply the knowledge they have gained as they work on an existing piece of writing.

Reflection:

Our curriculum frameworks in Arkansas, as well as most assessments (our state tests, AP Exams, etc.), demand that students exhibit control of the domain of style. As one aspect of style, we expect students to employ syntax purposefully. In this quick write, I am working with syntax in the context of a writer's workshop model: beginning with an explicit minilesson with models, allowing an opportunity for practice, and asking that students apply this concept in their own writing.

REFERENCES

Dickens, C. (1997). *A tale of two cities.* New York: Penguin.

King, S. (1990). *Carrie.* Garden City, NY: Doubleday

Salinger, J.(1966). *Catcher in the rye.* New York: Bantam.

Vidal, G. (1997). *Myra Breckinridge.* New York: Penguin.

Woolfe, V. (1925). *Mrs. Dalloway.* San Diego, CA: Harcourt.

Wouk, H. (1978) *The winds of war.* Boston: Little, Brown and Company.

"Round and Round We Go ..."

Jamie Highfill
8th- & 9th-Grade English Teacher,
Woodland Junior High School, Fayetteville, Arkansas

Directions:

All students should copy the sentence "All of a sudden, the principal's voice boomed over the intercom" onto their yellow pads. They should also put their names at the top of the page. *In a moment we're going to write a story using the sentence you've just written down, but WE'RE ALL going to write it. As soon as I say "Go," write as much as you can continuing from this starting point, until I say "Switch." Then you will pass your pad to the person on your left, who will read what you have written, and then continue from where you left off, and so on until I tell everyone to stop.*

Get students started, and let them have about 45 seconds to one minute on the first round before you tell them to "switch." After that, give them about a minute and a half to 3 minutes before you tell them to switch, then three minutes, etc. Go about 15 to 20 minutes and then have the students stop, and return the pads to their original owners.

Have students share some of their stories.

Reflection:

I've done write-arounds before and enjoyed doing them. I used this as a quick write lesson to teach my students sequencing and order. They loved it! Afterwards, I asked them what they found challenging about the write-around. They told me that it was hard to write and follow other people's thoughts in a logical sequence, so this was a perfect jumping off place to move on to discussing transitions in writing, and logical sequencing, etc.

They have asked me several times over the course of the year when we're doing it again. Hmmm ...

Into the Forest: Imitating the Writer's Craft

Shelley Dirst
Literacy Specialist,
Arkansas Department of Education

Directions:

Say: *Barbara Kingsolver is a bestselling author with an academic background in ecology and evolutionary biology. She is also a master of craft, consistently using vivid imagery and syntax to pull the reader into the scene. Listen to this excerpt from the first page of her novel,* The Poisonwood Bible:

> *First, picture the forest. I want you to be its conscience, the eyes in the trees. The trees are columns of slick, brindled bark like muscular animals overgrown beyond all reason. Every space is filled with life: delicate, poisonous frogs war-painted like skeletons … secreting their precious eggs onto dripping leaves. Vines strangling their own kin in the everlasting wrestle for sunlight. The breathing of monkeys. A glide of snake belly on branch. A single-file army of ants biting a mammoth tree into uniform grains and hauling it down to the dark for their ravenous queen. And, in reply, a choir of seedlings arching their necks out of rotted tree stumps, sucking life out of death. The forest eats itself and lives forever.*

After the reading, engage students in a discussion of the images that were most powerful to them. Then, make the text available to students and arrange the students in pairs. Have students identify the examples of vivid word choice and figurative language that Kingsolver uses to create her scene. Also, ask them to analyze the syntax, particularly the variety in sentence length, the intentional use of fragments, and the rhythm in her sentence formation.

Then, ask students to work independently in response to the following prompt. Say: *Select a place you know and can describe. For example, this could be the kitchen at the fast food restaurant where you work, the barn on your family farm, or the virtual landscape in a videogame. Now, use Barbara Kingsolver's writing as inspiration to take us into that place.*

Your students may need the support of copying Kingsolver's paragraph as a template in which they insert their own content. To guide them, provide a model: Say: *Let's write the first sentences together. I am creating a scene about a cave where I hiked last weekend. So, I'll begin this way:*

> *First, think of the darkest place you've ever been. I want you to imagine a cave, an empty space that towers over you. The walls are fortresses of slimy, living rock like arms holding back the earth above.*

Reflection:

I have used this quick write in various versions with teachers and students. I sometimes accompanied it with preteaching on "showing, not telling," using specific sentences from the book. I offered a simple sentence: *My sister Rachel was prissy.* I then offered Kingsolver's actual, vivid sentence: *Rachel walked with her hands held out slightly from her thighs as if she had once again, as usual, been crowned Miss America.* Another example is my simple sentence: *When the rain stopped, my sisters ran outside.* Kingsolver's actual version is this: *The world looked stepped on and drenched, but my sisters ran out squealing like the first free pigs off the ark, eager to see what the flood had left us.* Examining Kingsolver's craft made a real impression and helped students better grasp the power of the writer's craft.

REFERENCE

Kingsolver, B. (1998). *The poisonwood bible.* New York: Harper Collins.

Do You Hear What I Hear?

Clare Lesieur
K-4 Academic Coach,
Harrison School District, Harrison, Arkansas

Directions:

Read *Good-Night, Owl* by Pat Hutchins, or another book that features sound words (onomatopoeia). You can also sing "Old MacDonald Had a Farm." Make a list of sound words from the story/song on the board or on chart paper. Write a class poem using sound words from the story.

Brainstorm other sound words. You may choose to focus on one topic or several. Good topics for this activity include a farm, night, a pond, a theme park, the school bus, etc.

Once you have generated a good list or lists, ask students to write their own sound poems about one of the selected topics or one of their own.

Samples of Class-Generated Sound Poems:

Night
Howls, hoots
Wings that flap

Branches that clink
Scary sounds
Night sounds

Moo, oink,
Quack, quack, quack
Nay,
Nay,
Hear the animals?
Baby animals

Reflection:

I am always amazed at how naturally young children write poetry. They are not tied down by "the rules" yet. I usually need to have emerging writers read their writing to me. I record their responses and often type their writing for them. Students enjoy seeing their work in print and love to illustrate their own writing. Sound poems are especially engaging for young authors.

REFERENCE

Hutchins, P. (1990) *Good-night, owl*. New York: Simon & Schuster.

Five Senses

Clare Lesieur
K-4 Academic Coach,
Harrison School District, Harrison, Arkansas

Directions:

Read *Hello Ocean, Hola Mar* by Pam Munoz Ryan. Make a "five senses" chart on the board or overhead. List words from the book that fit into each category.

Put students into groups of five. Pass out "five senses" charts to each student with a place/event written at top of the page. Each student in the group should get a different topic, such as: birthday party, Christmas, picnic, swimming pool, football game, and so on. Set the timer for 30 seconds. Students are to fill in as many descriptive words as possible on their charts before time is called. Then, students rotate their papers within their groups. Add an additional ten seconds to each rotation, so students may read what the previous students have written before adding their own sensory words.

After five rotations, students should receive the page they started with. Ask students to return to their seats and write independently on the assigned topic using some of the words generated by the group. Allow time to share.

Reflection:

This lesson can be modified in many ways. Students can work on one topic together in small groups and share a group-written paragraph. Or, charts for each topic can be posted around the room, and once the class has brainstormed sensory words, students may select any posted topic to write about.

Extend the lesson by having students write about a favorite place using their five senses chart for prewriting.

Adapt this activity for younger students by having them write a five-senses riddle:

I hear the seagulls.
I see the blue water.
I feel a hermit crab's claw.
I taste sand in my mouth.
I smell a dead fish.

Where am I?

REFERENCE

Ryan, P. M. (2003). *Hello ocean, hello mar.* Watertown, MA: Charlesbridge.

When I Was Young in the Mountains

Mary Wince
Coordinator of Gifted Education,
Valley Springs School, Valley Springs, Arkansas

Directions:

Begin the quick write by introducing the book, *When I Was Young in the Mountains*. Ask the audience to listen as you read and notice the ways Cynthia Rylant uses sensory details to describe the everyday events of her mountain life. They should also be directed to listen for a refrain.

After reading the book aloud, discuss briefly the author's attention to sensory details and the refrain—when I was young in the mountains. Ask students to think about why the author chose to use the refrain intermittently rather than on each page. (Younger children are likely to use a refrain for each memory unless you discuss this prior to writing.)

After the above is completed, I say: *Now it's your turn. Write about your memories of the everyday events of childhood. Remember to use sensory details. You may want to create your own refrain and "sprinkle" it throughout your description. You will have 3 minutes to write.*

After the time expires, invite authors to share their childhood memories.

Reflection:

This quick write is especially appropriate as an introduction to memoir writing. Students in Grades 3–12 have little difficulty generating "growing-up" memories. In addition, this quick write frequently serves as a springboard for further writing. Students may want to focus and elaborate on an individual memory.

REFERENCE

Rylant, C. (1982). *When I was young in the mountains*. New York: Dutton.

Photo Memories

Rita S. Caver
10th-Grade Honors English Teacher,
Fayetteville High School, Fayetteville, Arkansas

Directions:

Tell the group that they are going to take a trip down memory lane. You might relate this to other exercises that they have done—thinking about their coveted possession or thinking about the treasures that they've written about. Show the group a photograph and tell them about the memories that come when you look at the photograph. Emphasize the vivid visual aspects of thinking of a photograph and the corresponding memories. Also emphasize the use of action verbs and clear nouns.

Each individual should then write a paragraph about an especially vivid memory that they have. They might want to shut their eyes and visualize the image. Give them 5 minutes. Do not have participants share at this point. Next, have individuals go back through the paragraph and circle the most vivid and the most significant words that they used. They should take the circled words and try to put the image in poetic form. After about 5 minutes, allow participants to share either piece.

Sample of student work:

The phone rang at 2:30 AM. Bad sign. The phone never rings at that time with good news. I would welcome a wrong number. Chad answered, listened, I even heard a quick intake of breath and a groan. The light was still off when he turned to me and said it was his dad and that my mother and father had been killed in a car accident. No, my parents were on their way to visit us in South Carolina and were stopping for the night somewhere in Georgia. We'll see them tomorrow. Through Chad, his father related how my parents had decided to drive straight through. About 10:00 PM, near Augusta, Georgia, a car had crossed the center lane. Mother was driving, approaching a bridge. There was no place to go. All were killed instantly. (Words and phrases that the student chose to circle are underlined.)

The phone rings at 2:30 AM
Chad answers
An intake of breath
A groan
There's been a car accident

Your folks
"No
We'll see them tomorrow."
No

Reflection:
My students especially like the move from prose to poetry. The second part of the exercise requires them to see if they did use vivid language. Most are successful with this and they enjoy having the option of reading either piece. My team teacher and I also do this writing activity.

Sweeter Than Kisses

Anita Philbrick
Reading Specialist,
Eunice Thomas Intermediate School, Cassville, Missouri

Directions:
I start by asking the group to think about chocolate. For example, I might say something along these lines: *Everybody loves chocolate. Oh, I suppose there are a few unfortunate people who do not enjoy savoring the feeling of rich, sweet chocolate as it melts in their mouths and runs down their throats. They, though, will never know the pleasure of a sundae oozing with syrupy, sticky, hot fudge on a hot summer afternoon or a nice pint of chocolate ice cream after a fight with a boyfriend.*

Then I say: *Chocolate assaults the senses. Unwrap the crinkly paper and a rich, dark aroma wafts through the air. Anticipation. Pop it in your mouth and feel the warm, smooth, sticky texture as it begins to melt. Pleasure. Finally, the taste. Lavish in its creaminess. M-m-m! No, chocolate is not a food; it is an experience.*

Next, I provide a synopsis of the book *Charlie and the Chocolate Factory*.

The main character, Charlie Bucket, lives in a ramshackle cottage in the same town as the mysterious Willie Wonka's Chocolate Factory. Although wonderful smells emanate from the factory, filling the town with the most marvelous smells a nose has ever inhaled, no one has ever seen anyone enter or leave the factory for many years. One day, Wonka announces that five lucky children and their families will tour his factory. The winners will be the finders of the five golden tickets hidden in Wonka Bars. This announcement causes a frenzy of candy bar buying throughout the entire world. Four bars are found quickly, but the last ticket is not discovered until the night before the end of the contest. Of course, Charlie is the fifth lucky winner. On March 1, 14 lucky people enter Wonka's factory for the first time in 10 years. The excerpt you are about to hear describes the first room they enter—the Chocolate Room, where all the chocolate is manufactured.

I explain to the students that since this book has few pictures, they will need to begin making pictures in their minds. For example, I say: *What does the room look like? How does it feel? What kinds of smells do you detect? Is the room warm or cold? What sounds do you hear? Do you taste anything?*

At this point, I give everyone a chocolate kiss in order to savor the texture, taste, and smell while the excerpt is read aloud. I then read the excerpt from Chapter 15 in *Charlie and the Chocolate Factory* to the students. After the excerpt is read, I provide the students with the following writing prompt:

You have all had some experience with chocolate in your lives. Describe how chocolate makes you feel or write about an experience you have had with chocolate (i.e., a birthday experience with chocolate cake, the time you first tasted chocolate, why you do or do not like chocolate). Use lots of sensory words to describe your experience with chocolate. You may use any format—story, poem, tall tale, limerick, conversation—that you wish. Write for 5 minutes. At the end of the 5 minutes those students who wish to share do so.

Reflection:

I use this activity as an extension to a unit on chocolate that I do in December. Of course, the children love to eat the chocolate. Almost always, they generate interesting stories and poems about their experiences and feelings about chocolate. I usually extend this activity by having them write sensory words on a chart as a prewriting activity. We publish their responses on large construction paper candy kisses. It's a sweet activity for all.

REFERENCE

Dahl, R. (1963). *Charlie and the chocolate factory.* New York: Puffin Books.

Meanwhile, Back at the Ranch

Mary Wince
Coordinator of Program for K–12 Gifted/Talented Students,
Valley Springs School, Valley Springs, Arkansas

Directions:

Rancher Hicks and his wife Elna live out west where nothing much ever happens. Rancher Hicks decides to drive into the town of Sleepy Gulch to see what's happening, while Elna stays at home to dig potatoes. While in town Rancher Hicks spends his day checking out 12-year-old wanted posters at the post office, listening to ancient gossip at the barber shop, eating at Millie's Mildew Luncheonette whose menu is composed exclusively of potato dishes, sitting in on the 2-week-old checker game at the general store, and watching the turtle cross Main Street. By the end of his day, Rancher Hicks is feeling extremely bad that Elna has missed all the excitement. Meanwhile, back at the ranch, Elna's day has been jam-packed with one exciting episode after another!

To begin the quick write, introduce the book *Meanwhile Back at the Ranch* by Trinka Hakes Noble. Ask the audience to notice how the author uses humor in the story. After reading aloud the book, discuss briefly the author's use of exaggeration and unexpected events to create humor. Then tell the group they will have 3–5 minutes to respond to the following prompt: *Using the "meanwhile, back at the ranch" format, write about what happens the next week when Elna goes to Sleepy Gulch while Rancher Hicks stays home, or perhaps you would like to make it more personal by writing about what might be happening back at your own "ranch" while you're sitting here in class. Try out the use of exaggeration and unexpected events to create humor in your writing today. Today's goal is to have fun. After 5 minutes of writing, I'll ask for volunteers to share their writing.*

Reflection:

Students of all ages love this book and enjoy continuing the saga of Rancher Hicks and his wife Elna who live just down the road (84 miles!) from Sleepy Gulch. With primary students, I have had the class create a group story using the format. Upper-level students enjoy working in small groups or writing their own versions. In middle school and high school, I have also used the following prompt with interesting results: *Due to extreme boredom, you play hooky from school. While you experience a rather mundane day, describe what happens. Use "meanwhile, back at school" as the story-starter.*

REFERENCE

Noble, T. H. (1992). *Meanwhile back at the ranch*. Hong Kong: Puffin Pied Piper Printing.

"Schoolsville"

Shelley Dirst
***10th-, 11th-, and 12th-Grade English Teacher,
Omaha High School, Omaha, Arkansas***

Directions:
"Welcome to My Reality!" This poster reminds us that it is the teacher who sets the climate of the classroom. However, as any student knows, each teacher has an individual persona and teaching style, whether it is the mother hen, the dictator, the salesman, or something else.

In the poem by U.S. Poet Laureate Billy Collins, the speaker reflects on his teaching career and envisions his role as a teacher in an unusual way. Listen carefully to what he has to say and how he says it:

"Schoolsville"

Glancing over my shoulder at the past,
I realize the number of students I have taught
Is enough to populate a small town.

I can see it nestled in a paper landscape,
Chalk dust flurrying down in winter,
Nights dark as a blackboard.

The population ages but never graduates.
On hot afternoons they sweat the final in the park
And when it's cold they shiver around stoves
Reading disorganized essays out loud.
A bell rings on the hour and everybody zigzags
In the streets with their books.

I forgot all their last names first and their
First names last in alphabetical order.
But the boy who always had his hand up
Is an alderman and owns the haberdashery.
The girl who signed her papers in lipstick
Leans against the drugstore, smoking,
Brushing her hair like a machine.

Their grades are sewn into their clothes
Like references to Hawthorne.
The A's stroll along with the other A's.
The D's honk whenever they pass another D.

All the creative writing students recline
On the courthouse lawn and play the lute.
Wherever they go, they form a big circle.
Needless to say, I am the mayor.
I live in the white colonial at Maple and Main.
I rarely leave the house. The car deflates
In the driveway. Vines twirl around the porchswing.

Once in a while a student knocks on the door
With a term paper fifteen years late
Or a question about Yeats or double-spacing.
And sometimes one will appear in a window pane
To watch me lecturing the wall paper,
Quizzing the chandelier, reprimanding the air.

Think of a metaphor to describe your favorite (or least favorite) teacher's persona and the relationship between him/her and the students he/she teaches. What is he or she?

Talk show host?
Circus ringmaster?
Fortune teller?
Horse whisperer?

Create your metaphor and free write for 10 minutes.

Reflection:
I created this quick write for use with teachers and was amazed by the insightful, poignant responses it elicited as these teachers reflected on their own personas. I believe this activity would be equally successful when adapted, as you see here, for students to write about their teachers. Collins' poem presents a vivid stimulus for teachers and students alike.

REFERENCE

Collins, B. (2001). Schoolsville. In *Sailing alone around the room: New and selected poems* (p. 18). New York: Random House.

Get in the Picture

Meredith Cox
1st–3rd-Grade Teacher,
Jones Elementary School, Springdale, Arkansas

Directions:
The following activity is a great way to teach students to use imagery and strong verbs in their writing. Collect interesting photographs (without captions) from magazines such as *National Geographic, Audubon,* and *Conde Nast Traveler.* One must have more than enough photographs available so each student can choose a photograph that piques his or her interest. Tell students to imagine they are the person taking the photograph, the subject in the picture, or someone who happened upon the setting. Comment on the point that some students may even think of a special memory when looking at a photograph. Remind students that they are "in the picture." Their task is to describe what they hear, feel, see, smell, and taste as they write about the photograph. Give the students 3–5 minutes to write, then ask volunteers to share their writing.

Reflection:
Before my students did this exercise the first time, I found it helpful to share a "photo essay" I had written. It seems to help get their writing juices flowing.

My fifth-grade students enjoyed this activity so much that they wanted to continue reading each other's stories. I glued their stories and photographs to construction paper and bound the pages together to form our own class book of "photo essays." Some students wrote plausible stories even though they interpreted the photographs differently from their actual content.

My Favorite Place

Helen Eaton
4th-Grade Teacher,
Holcomb Elementary School, Fayetteville, Arkansas

Directions:

Think about your favorite place. Think about a place that is special to you. It can be a place you've visited once, a place from your past, or a place you spend time in each day. Think about why you love this place. Think about the memories or comforts there. What do/did you see, hear, taste, smell, or feel there? Our best writing examples come from good literature. Listen and try to imagine each setting as I read aloud paragraphs rich in sensory language.

Some possible books to read selections from:

Number the Stars by Lois Lowery (p. 60) for sense of sight
Owl Moon by Jane Yolen (p. 3) for sense of hearing
Charlotte's Web by E. B. White (p. 13) for sense of smell
Pink and Say by Patricia Polacco (p. 10) for sense of touch
Little House in the Big Woods by Laura Ingalls Wilder (p. 152) for sense
   of taste

Think about what you see, hear, smell, taste, and feel at your own favorite place. Write a descriptive essay or paragraph about that place.

Note:

It is a good idea to let students use a yellow legal pad to write the essays. In the real world, grown-ups use these for taking notes, rough drafts, or jotting down ideas. When kids write on these, they know it is just a beginning, something to be changed, a "sloppy copy." Also, have students skip one or two lines between each line of writing to insert changes, add more, or even cut apart later.

Reflection:

I first began to use this quick write ("My Favorite Place") with my students because it was the district beginning-of-the-year prompt to be used with all fourth-grade students; however, it has become one of my favorite writing topics. As I read the children's paragraphs or essays describing their favorite places, I saw that this was a chance for them to write about something that was important to them, something about which they were the authorities. Their voices could be heard clearly even in rough drafts. I have found this to be an excellent piece to use to guide children through the entire writing process.

I have also used this quick write in several writing inservices with teachers. Adults also have a feeling of comfort to write about a subject that they love, a setting they can easily imagine. Often, thinking about a place dear to the heart brings back vivid memories, which can bring about equally vivid descriptive writing.

REFERENCES

Lowry, L. (1989). *Number the stars*. New York: Dell.

Polacco, P. (1994). *Pink and Say*. New York: Scholastic.

White, E. B. (1952). *Charlotte's web*. New York: HarperTrophy.

Wilder, L. I. (1932). *Little house in the big woods*. New York: HarperCollins.

Yolen, J. (1987). *Owl moon*. New York: Putnam.

The Most Beautiful, Exciting, or Exotic Place I've Ever Been

Samuel Totten
Founder and Director of the Northwest Arkansas Writing Project, and Professor of Curriculum and Instruction, University of Arkansas, Fayetteville

Directions:

I introduce this activity by saying something along the line of: *We've all either lived or visited some place that is special to us in a unique and powerful way. It may be due to the scenic beauty, the architecture, a combination of the latter, the setting itself (such as the ocean, mountains, desert), or a locale that brings back special memories.*

Personally, I've been extremely lucky in this regard for I've traveled fairly extensively across the globe. That's due in large part to the fact that my first teaching job was in Victoria, Australia. Later, I taught at the American School in Israel, and as a university professor I've had the opportunity to teach courses all over Central and South America, including Mexico, Colombia, Chile, Bolivia, Ecuador, Paraguay, and Honduras.

During the course of my travels what I love most is to discover what I consider exotic places—places that make me feel as if I'm in another world or experiencing another period in time. Such places are harder and harder to come by in this age of globalization when you can find, for example, a McDonald's along any major street in many far-off lands.

That said, some of the places I've visited were quite exotic. To show you what I mean I have a series of photos from each place I'm going to mention so that you can see what I mean.

First, there was, back in 1978, Kathmandu, Nepal. I flew into Kathmandu around midnight and when I woke up in the morning I was enchanted to find that I had landed in a kingdom that felt, looked, and smelled as if it were the Middle Ages. Yaks and cows roamed idly down the twisting, serpentine streets, munching on mounds of fresh vegetables that were stacked on the ground in front of open markets; Tibetan mountain men, with long pony tails and clothing made from hides, strode through the market with long knives dangling from their belts. Huge vats of steaming yak milk were boiled in open-air stalls and ladled out to cold and thirsty passersby.

Camping with nomadic Bushmen in the Kalahari Desert in the late 1970s. The men and women were naked except for jock-strap-like accouterments, and they lived out in the open where the small men hunted antelopes with small bows and arrows and the women foraged for melons with specially carved sticks. They slept under the stars, and constantly had a fire going on which to cook their meager meals and/or to keep warm by.

Walking through the suq (or open market) in Hebron, Palestine, in the early 1980s where the delicious smell of shalisk on a spit rose up in huge billows of smoke as I made my way down the dark cavern filled with tiny shops with men smoking hookahs and wearing keffiyahs.

Viewing the camel market in Rafa, Egypt, in the early 1980s, where the local Bedouins checked out the legs and feet of the camels and raced the camels up and down dirt roads as if they were buying a new car.

Buying goods in the suq in Abeche, Chad, in 2004, where the main modes of transportation were donkeys and camels, and Arab women with veils stared at me with their large, brown eyes.

OK, what I wish to have you do is quickly jot down the most exotic, exciting, or beautiful places you've ever been. It need not be exotic. Places that are breathtaking, exciting, or gorgeous are equally fine to write about. Try to come up with four or five places.

OK, now select one of those places and using the most vivid but exact words you can, paint a picture of that place. Make it so realistic that it transports the reader to the place you experienced in the way that you experienced it.

Provide time for three or four students to share what they've come up with.

Reflection:

This quick write is always a hit with students. They all seem to have a special place that they wish to write about. For many, it's a place close to their local community or a river or lake not far from home. For some, it's a place that they vacationed at with their parents—San Francisco, Washington, D.C., rafting down the Colorado River, the Grand Tetons, Yosemite, the first time they ever saw the ocean. I am frequently amazed by how well the students are able to create vivid pictures of those places that are special to them. Then again, maybe I shouldn't be, for they are writing from personal experience and about experiences that may have transformed, if not transported, them in some way.

My Town May Not Have "Big Shoulders," But It Has What Chicago Can Only Dream Of

Samuel Totten
Founder and Director of the Northwest Arkansas Writing Project, and Professor of Curriculum and Instruction, University of Arkansas, Fayetteville

Directions:

Provide the students with a copy of Carl Sandburg's poem "Chicago." Read it aloud with the passion that the poem itself exudes. Next, ask the students the following questions, discussing each in a fair amount of detail: *Is he honest or circumvent about its qualities? Evidence?; How does Sandburg perceive Chicago? Evidence? Does he have disdain for it or...? Evidence? Does he perceive it as an effete city or?*

Next, ask: *Are there any images that jump out at you, "grab you by the throat"? Or, as Emily Dickinson put it, "take off the top of your head" they're so powerful?* List these on the board as the students call them out.

Once the list is complete, ask the students why such images are so powerful.

Next, ask if there's anything in the poem the students don't understand, and quickly address such matters by asking the rest of the class what they think or by offering your own insights.

Finally, say, *OK, I want each of you to either write down the name of your favorite village, town, city in the world, your hometown (that is, where you were born), or the town in which you currently live. Once you do that, I simply want you to list its most vivid and significant attributes/components/aspects. As you do this really try to use phrases that are "showing, not telling." Once you have listed a good 10 or so attributes, I want you to create your own poem in which you convey your feelings and thoughts as strongly as Sandburg did in his writing of* Chicago.

Reflection:

I first tried this activity with my students at the U.S. House of Representatives Page School, where I was the English teacher. The 75 or so students represented close to 40 states, and since this was the first time they lived away from home for an extended period of time, many of them missed their hometowns. The writing that resulted from this activity was remarkable. The students, all 11th graders, wrote with passion, using astonishingly vivid images that provided us all with a clear sense of their hometowns or favorite cities in the world.

REFERENCE

Sandburg, C. (1916). *Chicago poems*. New York: Henry Holt.

Why I Prefer ...

Samuel Totten
Founder and Director of the Northwest Arkansas Writing Project, and Professor of Curriculum and Instruction, University of Arkansas, Fayetteville

Directions:

I've discovered that "breezy" or quirky articles in the newspaper as well as "snappy" advertisements are great fodder for quick write ideas. The following quick write is an idea I picked up an advertisement for Raisin Bran cereal. As you will see, the individual touting the cereal uses a lot of adjectives that vividly portray why he finds the cereal so delightful to his palate.

I begin by sharing the following with the students: *I'm going to read you a testimonial I came across recently in which a famous chef states why he is such a fan of Raisin Bran cereal. As I read his words, listen closely to both the reasons he gives for liking the cereal so much as well as the specific words he uses to describe his favorite cereal.*

Next, I read the advertisement:

Raisin Bran: Le Petit Dèjeuner of Champions
by
Jean-Georges Vongerichten

I love it. I like it because it's a quick breakfast—you just have to open the box! I like the chewy raisins, the crunchy cereal. With a sliced banana and some milk, it's the quickest great healthy breakfast. It's crunchy, chewy. There's only one brand, no? Kellogg's—that's the one we have. Banana. Milk. Always the same thing. I'm boring. I eat it about three times a week. I like it with milk and a cappuccino. I grew up eating croissants, but they don't give you much energy in the morning, and I think I just like Raisin Bran because it's very balanced and I like the texture.

Jean-Georges Vongerichten is the owner of five Manhattan restaurants, including Jean Georges

Next I say: *Take several minutes and write about your favorite dish (not meal, but dish). It can be your favorite dish for breakfast, lunch, or dinner. Use descriptive language so that we can gain your sense of appreciation, delectation, if you will.*

Reflection:

This is one of the quickest quick writes I've used. Most students do not have to think very long at all before coming up with their favorite dish. The writing is often humorous, vivid, and surprising. In fact, the surprising nature of what students write about is why students seem to like this quick write so much. I mean, how many people would include the following as favorite dishes for breakfast? Fried eggplant smothered in mozzarella; two slices of bread covered with chunky peanut butter and a heavy drizzle of brown sugar on top glazed to a golden brown under the broiler; a tofu sandwich on lightly toasted wheat bread garnished with a thick slab of goat cheese, a slice of crispy red onion, and mashed garbanzo beans. I'm not kidding!

How Creative Can You Get?
Crazy, Mixed-Up Story Starters

Clare Lesieur
4th-Grade Teacher,
Skyline Heights Elementary School, Harrison, Arkansas

Directions:

Choose three colors of labels. Assign a story element to each color. For example: red = character, blue = setting, yellow = problem. Allow each student to choose a colored label. (I have my students wear their labels on their hands.) Depending on the color of their labels, students must come up with a creative character, setting, or problem for a story. Anything goes! (You may need to give or elicit examples to get things started.)

Next, allow students to form groups of three. Groups should contain one of each colored label (one of each story element). Students combine their story elements to create story starters. As groups share their story starters with the class, ask one student to record them on the board or overhead. (The combinations are usually very humorous!)

Examples

Character	Setting	Problem
A green poodle	on the planet Zephron	can't find a date for the prom
A child genius	in a rocket	is trapped inside a cereal box

After a good list has been generated, ask students to return to their desks. Each student should compose a piece using one of the story starters.

Allow time for students to share their writing.

Variations and Suggestions:

Students can be assigned tasks/groups in other ways. One time I simply used dry erase pens and put a colored dot on each student's hand. You may find that students need to write down their creative story elements. This keeps them from changing their ideas once in their groups.

Discourage discussion between students prior to grouping. This eliminates the formation of groups around a topic or theme. Remember that the fun of the activity is in trying to write from a crazy, mixed-up story starter!

Materials:
Color-coded labels (Colored stars or other stickers work well, too.)

Chasing Rainbows

Mary Wince
Literacy Coach,
Bruno-Pyatt School, Eros, Arkansas

Directions:
You don't have to be a cat lover to be captivated by the simple descriptive text and vivid illustrations in the book *Cat's Colors* by Jane Cabrera. I introduce this quick write by displaying a new box of crayons and sharing my feelings as I explore the contents. My testimonial goes like this: *I love crayons—especially new crayons with no broken tips. I love how they smell—and how smooth they feel between my fingers. I love imagining what marvelous pictures the crayons will create. But what I love most of all are the colors—so many colors. What is my favorite color? Is it green— or purple— or red?* From the crayon box, I pull out several colors that appeal to me. *It's so hard to choose just one. In the book* Cat's Colors *by Jane Cabrera, Cat faces this same problem. Let's read to find out how Cat decides which color is his favorite.* On each two-page spread, Cat ponders a color in the form of a question and makes a personal connection.... "I'm Cat. What is my favorite color? ... Is it Black? Black is the night when bats swoop and soar.... Is it Purple? Purple is the yarn I tangle in my claws...." On the final page, Cat reveals his favorite color with a special connection.

After reading the book, briefly discuss how Cat decides which color is his favorite. Then share the following prompt: *Now it's your turn. Write about your favorite color. If you are like Cat, you may want to write about more than one color, and you might want to save your favorite until last. Don't forget to tell why each color is special to you.* After a brief time, invite several students to share. Students who have not had an opportunity to share with the entire group may turn to someone sitting near them to share.

Samples of Writing From Kindergarten Students:

What is my favorite color?

Is it yellow?
Yellow is a fuzzy duckling chasing bugs in the grass.

Yellow is the NASCAR zooming down the track.
Yellow is the banana for my Cheerios.

Is it green?
Green is my dad's tractor plowing up the field.
Green is sour apple bubble gum.
Green is the tree we decorate at Christmas.

Is it red?
Red is the soft cozy teddy bear Grandma gave me to cheer me up.
Red is the lipstick on Momma's mouth.
Red is the bouncy rubber ball we kick in gym class.

Samples From 5th and 6th Grade Students:

Green
Green is the color
That lights the world
It's on the ground
Even in my eye

Green is the taste
We all have eaten.
The Granny Smith we might find
In the gleaming Emerald City.

When you see green,
You'll never forget
The color that favors
The fresh cut grass,
The smell of pine tar,
And the crack of a bat.

Yellow
Yellow is a newborn chick
The bright sun in the sky
Yellow tastes like banana nut bread
And feels like dandelion fuzz
Yellow is a radiant color

Pretty in Pink
Pink dresses with Pink ponytail holders
Pink stockings with Pink dress shoes
Pink sunglasses with Pink purses
Pink lipstick with Pink eye shadow

Pink pencils with Pink grippers

Pink paper with Pink crayons
Pink books with Pink bookmarks
Pink laptops with Pink backgrounds

Reflection:

This quick write is especially appropriate for students in grades K-3. To lift the quality of writing of young students, consider briefly discussing author's craft before providing the writing prompt. Students readily identify the pattern throughout the book—a question with a color word followed by a personal connection with some description. Like me, you may discover that students in kindergarten and first grade benefit from brief teacher modeling with a think aloud. For the very young students, I stick with the basic colors since color words are often displayed as a spelling aid on color charts or word walls in classrooms. However, for older students, feel free to play around with a broader palette: magenta, chartreuse, tangerine, burnt sienna. Don't forget to pair up with the art teacher—or strike out on your own—and encourage students to create colorful illustrations using crayons, markers, watercolors or tempera paint to accompany their writing. The bold illustrations in *Cat's Colors* will provide the inspiration.

For older students, try this quick write by sharing several poems from Mary O'Neill's timeless classic *Hailstones and Halibut Bones: Adventure in Color.* The text structure is similar to *Cat's Colors* in that the title of each color poem is in the form of a question. However, the content is far more complex. Both books easily serve as anchor texts, introducing young authors to the crafting technique of framing a question. Students can revisit these texts when exploring other topics, enabling them to envision possibilities for future writing. As an added bonus, O'Neill gives a fascinating account of how her book came to be in the introduction. This quick write is ideal to integrate with a science study of light, prisms and the spectrum.

One more book that's simply too good to pass up is *Color Me a Rhyme: Nature Poems for Young People* by Jane Yolen with photographs by Jason Stemple. On each two-page spread, this mother-and-son team explores a basic color by blending a poem, a quote, and a nature photograph. The pages are bordered by graphics of extra color words, thus providing a built-in thesaurus. The result is anything but basic. A note from the author describes the process of this collaboration and invites the reader to choose a photo and write. Provide the stimulus for a quick write by sharing a few poems with the accompanying photos. If you're lucky enough to have a friend who dabbles in nature photography, why not use your own photos—or "borrow" some from a nature photography book? I'm thinking of the perfect book on my shelf—*Arkansas Spring: Dogwoods, Waterfalls and Wildflowers* by Tim Ernst. Who knows? Your students may be inspired to grab a camera, capture some nature photographs—and write.

REFERENCES

Cabrera, J. (1997). *Cat's colors.* New York: Dial.

Ernst, T. (2000). *Arkansas spring: Dogwoods, waterfalls and wildflowers.* Pettigrew, AR: Cloudland.net

O'Neill, M. (1961). *Hailstones and halibut bones: Adventures in color.* New York: Delacorte Press.

Yolen, J. (2000). *Color me a rhyme: Nature poems for young people.* Honesdale, PA: Wordsong.

From Mrs. Malaprop to Archie Bunker to ...: Malapropisms

Samuel Totten
Founder and Director of the Northwest Arkansas Writing Project and Professor of Curriculum and Instruction, University of Arkansas, Fayetteville

Directions:
The teacher should inform his/her students of the following:

A malapropism is an instance of an individual using an entirely incorrect word in an or statement or written sentence that sounds like its correct counterpart, such as, "He's always using hypodermic statements" when what the speaker meant to say was: "He's always using hyperbolic statements."

In 1775, Richard Sheridan, a famous playwright, created a character named Mrs. Malaprop who had a tendency to badly mix up her use of words by using a similar-sounding word for the word she intended to use. The upshot was that her comments not only did not make sense, but were incredibly funny without her intent of being funny. Her name was taken from the French term "mal a propos," which basically means "inappropriate."

A more recent example of a fictional character who was wont to using malapropisms was Archie Bunker in the then famous television show "All in the Family." For example, he was known to say such things "All you get when you speak to her is condensation" when he meant to say "All you get when you speak to her is condescension."

In the next 5 minutes create your own character who is wont to using malapropisms. The piece need not be a story, but simply a vivid character sketch that includes dialogue in which one of the characters uses malapropisms.

Reflection:

Students seem to love this quick write since it is largely pure fun. Not only does it prod them to think about the correct usage of language but how the study and use of language can be thoroughly enjoyable. The joy for the teacher is that long after the use of this quick write students enjoy sharing examples of malapropisms that they have heard on the radio, television, in everyday speech, or on the Internet.

The Bite of Satire

Samuel Totten
Founder and Director of the Northwest Arkansas Writing Project
and Professor of Curriculum and Instruction,
University of Arkansas, Fayetteville

Directions:

Play one of the many classic songs by Tom Lehrer. I strongly recommend "We'll All Go Together When We Go," a song about the dangers of nuclear weapons and nuclear warfare. Several stanzas provide one with a sense of Lehrer's talent and satirical ability:

> When you attend a funeral
> It is sad to think that sooner or later
> Those you love will do the same for you
> And you may have thought it tragic
> Not to mention other adjec-
> Tives, to think of all the weeping they will do
> But don't you worry

> No more ashes, no more sackcloth
> And an armband made of black cloth
> Will someday never more adorn a sleeve
> For if the bomb that drops on you
> Gets your friends and neighbors too
> There'll be nobody left behind to grieve

And we will all go together when we go
What a comforting thought that is to know.
Universal bereavement, an inspiring achievement
Yes, we will all go together when we go

(NOTE: Many, if not most, of the songs are readily available on the Internet.)

Once the song has played, ask the students what they thought the song was about. As the students share their insights the teacher should help to provide a context for the time period that Lehrer was writing about. (Such information is also available on most Web sites that discuss Lehrer's work.)

Tell the students: *Instead of writing a serious essay Tom Lehrer used humor and satire to comment on the world at the time.*

Ask the students if they answer familiar with any authors, songwriters, newspaper editorialist, rappers who use satire to convey their sense of a situation. As they share, be sure to ask them to clarify how the example constitutes satire. (Some teachers may need to explain what satire is before asking for such examples.)

Next, ask the students to write their own satirical piece about the world in which they live and/or those issues that they perceive as world shaking. Tell them that it is easiest to do by selecting an issue they feel strongly about. (At this point it may be wise to either play the same song over again or another one by Lehrer or a more contemporary singer. This will provide studies with more insights as to how to write a satirical piece.)

Once the students have completed their quick writes allow those who wish to share to do so.

Reflection

This is a very popular quick write with students from about seventh grade up to the university level. Not only do they appreciate Lehrer's sense of black humor but appreciate the opportunity to let fly with their own satirical insights. This is an excellent quick write to use in an English class when teaching about satire and/or in and English or social studies class when talking about social issues and the use of satire to critique and/or condemn certain policies, incidents, events, personages, ideas.

For the Love of SPAM!

Norm Doege
High School English Teacher,
Bentonville High School, Bentonville, Arkansas

Directions:

If you have access to the SPAM Sketch by the Monty Python comedy troupe, play an audio or video clip of it. If not, then go ahead and simply "introduce" students to an actual can of SPAM and inform them that they will write some haikus about the delightful luncheon meat. A quick review of the haiku format—three lines following the 5–7–5 syllable format—may be needed. Share some published SPAM haiku to the class. Then, ask that the students be very quiet. They will need to open up their senses to the experience ahead. Carefully open the SPAM can (the edges can be sharp) and let it slide onto a plate. Cut it into chunks and serve it to students on toothpicks. Students should then compose their haikus. Remind them to use their senses: taste, smell, sound, vision, and touch. Give the students about 5 minutes or so to create. Allow them to share when they are done.

Reflection:

I have only tried this once during a creative writing class, but I believe it will work at any level. SPAM is a galvanizing subject; people either love it or hate it. The odd nature of the topic, combined with the presentation, encourages students to be silly and have fun. If a student so chooses, he or she can submit his or her effort to the online SPAM Haiku Archive. An instructor can adapt this lesson to work with more traditional objects such as hard candies. A warning: Don't try this unless you can go with the joke.

REFERENCES

SPAM Haiku Archive. (n.d.) http://pemtropics.mit.edu/~jcho/spam/
The SPAM Homepage. (n.d.) http://www.spam.com/
Cho, J. (Ed.). (1998). *SPAM-Ku: Tranquil reflections on luncheon loaf.* New York: HarperPerennial.
Monty Python's Flying Circus. (1970, December 12). "Spam"—Episode 25.

TIES TO LITERATURE

A Gift From the Heart

Samuel Totten
*Founder and Director of the Northwest Arkansas Writing Project
and Professor of Curriculum and Instruction,
University of Arkansas, Fayetteville*

Directions:

Read O'Henry's "Gift of the Magi" to the students (it's only about two and a half pages long). Then, without any discussion, have the students write a story when either they or someone they knew gave something extremely precious they owned to someone else out of great admiration and/or love. Or, if students have never given such a gift they can write about their being a recipient of such a gift. Note: If students have never given such a gift or been a recipient of one, then they should be given the opportunity to write about a person who they would one day give such a get to and why—and, if they have any idea as to what such a gift would be they should be encouraged to mention it and comment on why they would choose that particular gift.

Spark the Brain, Ignite the Pen: Quick Writes for Kindergarten Through High School Teachers and Beyond, 2nd Edition, pp. 131–141

Reflection:
"Gift of the Magi" is a story that most students—no matter how immature or jaded they are—will never forget. Responding to the story in a quick write is also likely to be an experience that stays with them a long time—that is, the essence of what they wrote, and why.

REFERENCE

O'Henry (2003). *The gift of the Magi and other stories*. New York: Scholastic.

What? Me Scared?

Rebecca Cantey
10th-Grade English Teacher,
Bentonville High School, Bentonville, Arkansas

Directions:
Say to the students: *Suspense is the growing feeling of anxiety and excitement that makes a reader curious about the outcome of the story. Suspense was built in Poe's "Masque of the Red Death" by the ominous clock tolling the hours in the seventh room with the blood red windows. Suspense was built in Poe's "The Pit and the Pendulum" when the prisoner, sentenced to death, finds himself in a pitch black room wondering what waits for him in the dark.*

We could not have suspense without fear. According to Rita Marie Keller, "Fear is the main element of successful horror fiction. Fear is what motivates writers such as Stephen King to pen these stories. King has admitted to being afraid of the dark.... He uses his own fear in his own work." Keller goes on to quote Shirley Jackson: "I have always loved to use fear, to take it and comprehend it and make it work and consolidate a situation where I was afraid and take it whole and work from there ... I delight in what I fear."

Share your own list with the students. For example:

Being in an enclosed place with no way out (elevator, coffin, etc.)
Being in the water when something starts nibbling at my toes
Forgetting to pick up my child from school
Throwing up in a public place
Going into labor and not being able to get to the hospital

Say: *Take a moment to list your recurring fears or haunting images. Now, choose one fear from your list and write about it for ten minutes.*

Reflection:

I have used this as a quick write in English II American Literature for several years during a Romanticism unit before we read "The Pit and the Pendulum." This quick write helped to set the mood of the piece—plus students love writing about what scares them. I had almost 100% participation in sharing this quick write. The quality of the writing was outstanding. My students demonstrated a better understanding of mood after this quick write which they used to expand into an essay about mood. I plan on using this quick write any time I use "The Pit and the Pendulum."

REFERENCE

Keller, R. M. (n.d.). *The darker side of writing: Creative exercises for horror writing.* Retrieved from www.geocities.com/rsw-news/horrorexercises.html

Is "No Man an Island" or ...?

Samuel Totten
Founder and Director of the Northwest Arkansas Writing Project and Professor of Curriculum and Instruction, University of Arkansas, Fayetteville

Directions:

Place the following quote on the overhead.

John Donne, the Metaphysical Poet, wrote that

No Man Is An Ilande, entire of it self; every man is a piece of the Continent, a part of the maine; if a Clod be washed away by the Sea, Europe is the lesse, as well as if a Promontorie were, as well as if a Mannor of thine friends or of thine owne were; any man's death diminishes me, because I am involved in Mankinde; And therefore never send to know for whom the bell tolls; It tolls for thee.

Say: *This famous statement is now used as an argument for "solidarity" amongst all people across the globe. To this day, many find solace in Donne's sentiments and believe that what he says is true. Many also believe that one can find plenty of actions in today's world that provide proof that such a sentiment is "alive and well." Other people, however, are not so sanguine. They argue that the world is far too big to feel such "solidarity" for everyone across the globe. They also point out that people who believe in or live under different political systems, believe in radically different religions, and/or come from very different cultures have little affinity with one another and that there is no way that Donne's sentiments are applicable in today's world.*

Do you agree or disagree with Donne's assertion/sentiments, and why or why not? In responding, please be sure to do your best to provide concrete examples from current society and your own life to support your position.

Reflection:

This quick write would be ideal to revise somewhat and use in either and/or an English, history, social studies or government course. Indeed, this is an excellent quick write to use in an English class when studying any number of literary works, both nonfiction and fiction (e.g., Griffin's *Black Like Me*, Hersey's *Hiroshima*, Steinbeck's *Of Mice and Men* and *Grapes of Wrath*, Hemingway's *A Farewell to Arms* and *For Whom The Bell Tolls*, Heller's *Catch 22*, Gaines' *The Autobiography of Miss Jane Pittman*). It is also an outstanding quick write to use in a social studies or government class when the students are studying about certain key events (e.g., any catastrophic event, the women's movement, the civil rights movement, the tragedy of 911).

Machiavelli's Descendents

Shelley Dirst
Literacy Specialist,
Arkansas Department of Education

Directions:

This quick write was conducted in preparation for studying an excerpt from Machiavelli's *The Prince*. It builds upon an anticipation guide designed to stimulate deeper thinking about the reading by asking students to reflect on and discuss their beliefs about key ideas suggested in the text. Say: *Let's begin our study of Machiavelli by using an anticipation guide to get us thinking about the big ideas. You will note your reactions to each statement and then follow up with a small group discussion.*

Anticipation Guide: *The Prince*

In this 1513 treatise on the qualities a prince must have to maintain his power, Machiavelli reveals the pragmatic (and, to many, cynical) philosophy that has become known as "Machiavellian." Before reading this text, examine each of the statements below and consider whether you agree or disagree with each.

Write **agree** or **disagree** beside each statement:

____ 1. It is better for a leader to be loved than to be feared.
____ 2. It is important for a political leader to keep his word to the people.
____ 3. Preserving peace should be a leader's primary concern.
____ 4. Sometimes a leader must use questionable means to maintain power.
____ 5. Most people are honest.

Small group discussion: Use your responses to the above statements as a basis for discussion. Also consider what connections you can make to our current political climate.

Following the anticipation guide activity, I ask students to do the following quick write based on relevant quotes from other sources. Say: *Here are a few famous quotes that pertain to the central issues we have been discussing today. I will read each one and pause briefly for you to think about whether this quote means something to you in light of our discussion. Select the ONE quote that interests you most. Write about it. You may want to explain the meaning of the quote, discuss whether you agree or disagree with the assertion, make connections to your experience, etc.*

Quick Write: *The Prince*

Choose ONE of the following quotes and write a response in light of our discussion:

- If you treat men the way they are, you never improve them. If you treat them the way you want them to be, you do. *(Goethe)*
- In the long run, every government is the exact symbol of its people, with their wisdom and unwisdom. *(Thomas Carlyle)*
- Tyranny is always better organized than freedom. *(Charles Peguy)*
- Almost all of our relationships begin, and most of them continue, as forms of mutual exploitation. *(W.H. Auden)*

After writing time is over, have students choose the strongest or most interesting point from their response. Allow them to share.

Reflection:

In addition to working with adult audiences, I used these activities with high school juniors and seniors to begin a study of Machiavelli. Of course, these activities merely represent the initial preparation and do not attempt to provide the historical context for this study. This particular content is applicable for social studies and humanities classes; however, *the process of using the anticipation guide and applicable quotes certainly translates across the curriculum.* Both activities generated high levels of student engagement, which made the subsequent reading of a very difficult text much more approachable. I am continually impressed by the role that pre-reading activities play in student motivation and in students' comprehension of material.

REFERENCE

Machiavelli, N. (1996). *The prince* (P. Sonnino, Trans.) Amherst, New York: Humanity Books.

Stories for Bear:
Launching the Reading and
Writing Workshops

Mary Wince
Literacy Coach,
Bruno-Pyatt School, Eros, Arkansas

Clare Lesieur
Academic Coach,
Harrison School District, Harrison, Arkansas

Directions:

Here's the perfect quick write to launch your reading and writing workshops. Share the book *A Story for Bear* by Dennis Haseley—a fantasy to celebrate the wonders of reading. One warm afternoon a bear discovers a letter tucked among the leaves on the forest floor. The fragment of paper leads him to a cabin and an unlikely friend—a human friend. Each day the bear returns to the cabin and watches from behind the pine trees as a woman sits in her chair and reads from a book. Little by little the bear overcomes his shyness and moves closer and closer to the woman until one day he finds himself resting at her feet. She opens her book and softly begins to read to him. The bear returns, day after day, all summer, and each night he carries the sound of her stories back to his cave. Then one brisk fall day, the bear arrives at the cabin to discover that his friend has gone. In her usual place in the yard she has left piles of her books with a note—*For my Bear.* Bear tenderly carries the books back to his den, and all that winter, until his friend returns in the spring, Bear remembers the sound of her voice reading to him.

After sharing the book, give the following prompt: *In the story, Bear's friend leaves behind books for her Bear—books to keep him company all through the winter. Think about the books that you love—books that you could not live without—books that have made you laugh or cry or have sent shivers down your spine—books that have taught you an important lesson or helped you learn some valuable information. Now which of these would you choose to add to Bear's pile? Write about your choice or choices. If you prefer, write a letter to Bear and tell him about the book(s) you are leaving for him.* After a brief time, invite several students to share. Students who have not had an opportunity to share with the entire group may turn to someone sitting near them to share.

Reflection:

Students of all ages, in fact anyone who has ever been read to, will find *A Story for Bear* simply irresistible. As codirectors of a 9-day summer writing workshop for teachers, we have shared this book with great success and used it to spark a book celebration. We gather around a table, each participant with a beloved book in hand—a book to share with Bear. We darken the room, light the candles, and begin to share the deep connections we have with books. As we listen, we jot down titles and authors—books to add to our personal wish lists. It's a great opportunity to put into motion what educator/author Lucy Calkins describes as a ritual designed to strengthen the bonds within a community of writers.

In the classroom, this quick write paired with a celebration of books is the ideal way to launch reading and writing workshops, explore literary histories and introduce students to book talks. Consider scheduling book celebrations throughout the school year. You might even extend invitations to other staff members such as the principal, literacy coach, media specialist, cooks...and don't forget parents, grandparents, friends, and community members. You get the picture. For those elementary classrooms with stuffed animal mascots, students can choose books to share with the mascot in lieu of Bear—or along with Bear. The use of a friendly letter format for this quick write lends an intimate touch to the writing.

There are many possible text-to-text connections. After reading the Newbery Award-winning book, *The Giver,* by Lois Lowry, as a literature circle book or a class novel, share the following prompt: *In Jonas' community, each family has access to only three books chosen by the Committee of Elders. Imagine that you have access to only three books for the rest of your life, but you may choose which three. Think about which books have had an impact on your life. Perhaps a particular book has entertained you, helped you solve a problem or taught you something new. Perhaps a book has encouraged you to consider ideas you've never thought of before. Perhaps you have loved a book so much that you could read it again and again. Which books would you* not *want to live without?*

In the opening scene of the movie *Forrest Gump,* Forrest sits on the bench waiting for a bus. As he waits, a floating feather comes to rest along Forrest's shoe. Forrest picks it up, opens his suitcase, and tucks the feather safely inside his beloved copy of *Curious George.* After students view the scene, use the following prompt: *Which book would you choose to tuck safely in your suitcase as your traveling companion? Write about a significant book in your life?*

REFRENCES

Calkins, L. (1994). *The art of teaching writing*. Portsmouth, NH: Heinemann.

Finerman, W., Tisch, S., Newrith, C. (Producers), & Zemeckis, R. (Director). (1994). *Forrest Gump* [Film]. Paramount Pictures.
Haseley, D. (2002). *A story for bear.* Orlando, FL: Harcourt.
Lowry, L. (1993). *The giver.* Boston: Houghton Mifflin.

Famous First Lines

Samuel Totten
Founder and Director of the Northwest Arkansas Writing Project
and Professor of Curriculum and Instruction,
University of Arkansas, Fayetteville

Directions:

Place a half a dozen famous first lines from famous literature works on the overhead, and read each:

"I am a sick man ... I am a spiteful man" from Dostovesky's *Notes from the Underground.*

"It was the best of times, it was the worst of times, it was the age of wisdom, it was the age of foolishness, it was the epoch of belief, it was the epoch of incredulity, it was the season of Light, it was the season of Darkness, it was the spring of hope, it was the winter of despair" from Charles Dicken's *A Tale of Two Cities*

"I had the story, bit by bit, from various people, and, as generally happens in such cases, each time it was a different story" from Edith Wharton's *Ethan Frome*

"If you really want to hear about it, the first thing you'll probably want to know is where I was born, and what my lousy childhood was like, and how my parents were occupied and all before they had me, and all that David Copperfield kind of crap, but I don't feel like going into it, if you want to know the truth" from J.D. Salinger's *Catcher in the Rye*

"In the town, there were two mutes and they were always together" from Carson McCuller's *The Heart is a Lonely Hunter*

Then tell the students it is their turn to take a shot a writing a memorable first line of a short story, play, or novel. The key is to make it interesting, unique, catchy, and above, all, memorable. It must also, of course, be tied in an integral way to the literary work's plot or theme.

Reflection:

This quick write is probably most ideal for students in advanced writing or advanced literature classes for they may be more likely and apt to have a deeper understanding, appreciation of literature and the significance of first lines, foreshadowing, symbolic structure, motifs, and so on. Ideally, the students have also already written a fair amount so that they have an idea for a short story, one act play or longer work.

Playing with language in this way helps students appreciate the power of language, the power of a phrase or sentence or two that is/are succinct, and the power of a riveting sentence, thought or idea to captivate a reader's interest at the outset of a piece of writing.

Dear Author

Samuel Totten
***Founder and Director of the Northwest Arkansas Writing Project
and Professor of Curriculum and Instruction,
University of Arkansas, Fayetteville***

Directions:

This is a simple but effective quick write that is ideal for use with students in middle school through graduate school. It is an activity that prods each student to seriously consider how a book may have impacted, in any way whatsoever, his or her perception of him- or herself, others, or the world in which he or she resides.

The teacher should select two to three of the shortest and most highly engaging letters (or put another way, letters that his or her students are most likely to find engaging)—from *Dear Author: Students Write About the Books That Changed Their Lives*, and read them aloud to the students. The students should be directed to listen carefully to each letter, noting how the letter writers, young people like themselves, are very specific in regard to how the book by the author they are writing to actually impacted their (the young people's) lives. While listening to the letters being read, the students should be directed to think about and jot down the titles of those books that changed or impacted their own lives in some important way.

Once the letter(s) has/have been read, the students should be informed that the letters should be fairly short, very specific, and include both a salutation and a closing. The students should be given 5–7 minutes (or a bit more, if needed) to write their letters. After writing the letters, those who wish to share should do so. Next every student (whether he or she read his or her piece aloud or not) could be asked to simply share the title of the book that he or she wrote about.

Those students who wish to actually send their letters to "their" author should be encouraged to develop the letter more fully, if need be, and then revise, edit, and polish it before sending it off.

Reflection:

Most people (including young students) have one or more books that they love. Many, however, do not seem to ponder how a particular book may have impacted their lives. This quick write prods students to reflect on the power of books, the joy of reading, and the importance of reading—especially as it relates to one's own life. The latter becomes very clear once students begin to share their letters.

Not only is this quick write a wonderful way to allow students to share something about their favorite books, but it is a great way for students to be introduced to and to learn about books that they might not otherwise be familiar with. In that regard, it is a good way to build on the students' enjoyment and excitement about reading.

Finally, this quick write can be expanded into a more formal classroom exercise/activity. In that regard, the students can be given much more time to write their letters, share their letters in response groups or with a partner, get feedback, revise and, ultimately, edit their letters. At the conclusion, they are able to actually mail the letters to the authors to whom they are addressed. In that sense, this activity involves many aspects of process writing and involves writing for a real audience for a specific purpose. In other words, the entire activity becomes one that is "authentic." For some lucky students, it also means receiving a letter from their favorite author.

REFERENCE

Weekly Reader Magazine Staff. (1995). *Dear author: Students write about the books that changed their lives.* Berkeley, CA: Conari Press.

MATH

Talk Geometry to Me!

Pam Mulson
Elementary Math Coordinator,
Fort Smith Public Schools, Fort Smith, Arkansas

Directions:

I always like to tell the story to my students about Gracie Allen and George Burns. First, I have to explain who these people are because most young people are unfamiliar with these classic comedians.

I relate the story of Gracie observing her daughter working her geometry homework. The daughter sighs in exasperation, "Learning geometry is like learning a new language!" Gracie says, "Oh, talk geometry to me!" So the daughter replies, "Pi are square" (πr^2). To which Gracie replies, "Oh that is silly, everyone knows pies are round!"

Kids think the story is corny but it makes a point that learning the math vocabulary is like learning a new language.

Say, *Some say, "Geometry is like another language." Explain what you think this statement means.*

Reflection:

I gave this writing prompt early in my career as a classroom teacher and only because my principal was requiring more writing in the content areas. So, I just thought this might be interesting to try. When I received the responses, I was amazed at the analogies that the students made between learning a new language and learning geometry. It became a pivotal moment for me in my approach to teaching mathematics. It sold me on the power of writing to learn.

Spark the Brain, Ignite the Pen: Quick Writes for Use in Kindergarten Through High School and Beyond, 2nd Edition, pp. 145–158

What's Your Sign?

Kristen Scanlon
Director of Federal Programs,
Fayetteville Public Schools, Fayetteville, Arkansas

Directions:

This activity helps students realize the important role symbols play in mathematics. Mathematicians think in symbols, but it is confusing for students who are often faced with many symbols that are hard to understand or difficult to relate to the mathematics behind them. Students need to learn to recognize and interpret symbols so that they become part of their math language.

Show the students a grade-appropriate list of math symbols and their corresponding meanings: 0, 1, 2, 3, 4, 5, 6, 7, 8, 9, +, -, x, ÷, ≠, <, ≤, >, ≥, \$, %, :, π, ..., _, Σ, ∞, ≈, and so on. Discuss these with students, and ask the students for their ideas on how some of the symbols may have been developed. For example, you could explain that Robert Records developed the equal sign in the sixteenth century for his book *Whetstone of Whitte*. He said that he chose two parallel lines of equal length because no two things could be more alike. Students may work individually or in small groups.

Writing Activity

1. Invent a math symbol. Tell how to use it and when to use it.
2. Define the symbol carefully, including an explanation and a definition.
3. Develop several examples to show how to use it.
4. Write a set of four practice problems to test whether other students can use the new symbol correctly.
5. Share symbols with the class.

Sample of Student Work:

"My symbol is the division symbol with a circle around it. It means that a division problem comes out evenly without a remainder."

Reflection:

This activity is a good one to use prior to introducing a new math symbol. It helps students to connect symbols to the mathematical relationships they represent, and it also gives creative students a chance to shine.

REFERENCES

History of mathematics. (n.d.). Retrieved from http://math.about.com/od/history/History_of_Mathematics.htm

Math and number symbolism. (n.d.). Retrieved from http://www.symbols.net/math/

Some common mathematical symbols and abbreviations (with history). (2007). Retrieved MONTH, DATE, YEAR, from http://www.math.ucdavis.edu/~issy/teaching/s07/mat22a/mat22a-1_s07-common_math_Symbols.pdf

Weaver, D. (n.d.). *The history of mathematical symbols.* Retrieved from http://www.roma.unisa.edu.au/07305/symbols.htm

Web-based references for the history of math symbols. (n.d.). Retrieved from http://members.aol.com/jeff570/mathsym.html

Word Connections

Pam Mulson
Elementary Math Coordinator
Fort Smith Public Schools, Fort Smith, Arkansas

Directions:

Students are given a list of vocabulary words for the unit currently being studied. Say: *Look up the nonmathematical meaning of each of these words. The words should not be math related! Choose a definition that speaks to you and has meaning for you. You may not necessarily have the same definition as your neighbor. Now choose five to ten of the words you defined and write a short story using the words in context and in a way that makes sense. Underline the vocabulary words used.*

Sample of Student Writing Response:

The gold <u>circle</u> on her finger was slowly slipping off. She didn't notice because she was concentrating on her posture. She was nearly <u>perpendicular</u>. The <u>radius</u> of her arm ached because of the load she was carrying. In the <u>center</u> of her forehead, between her eyes, was a small symbol. A loud voice <u>ordered</u> the <u>system</u> of people to take the sacks towards the <u>slope</u> into the next room. The <u>geometry</u> of the room was odd but inspiring. The ring on her finger was nearly off, still unnoticed by her. A <u>form</u> of a human walked in among them, thoroughly covered with robes of silk and lathered with jewels. The people seemed to freeze and were erect. The gold ring finally fell off, but the man next to her <u>intercepted</u> it making the highly dressed person glare at him, at once informing the man with the loud voice to kill this slave. Before being seized, he slipped the precious jewel into her hand. Her eyes said thank you.

Reflection:

This writing idea came from Karen Brooks, a fellow Northwest Arkansas Writing Project Teacher Consultant and colleague in my district. She is always sharing her great lessons. An idea she generated was one in which students are helped to see the connection between the mathematical meaning and the everyday use of the words or vocabulary used in mathematics. The student that wrote the above piece was very quiet and rarely spoke in class. Writing gives every student a voice and uncovers hidden talent and untapped potential.

Rubber Band Words

Pam Mulson
Elementary Math Coordinator,
Fort Smith Public Schools, Fort Smith, Arkansas

Directions:

List a common mathematical term, such as fractions, polygons, circles, whole numbers, and so on. Have students write an acrostic that describes the word or concept. I call these "rubber band" words because you are expanding or stretching the word out.

Samples:

"Fractions"

Fragments
Rearranged
All
Combined
To
Ingulf
One
Nice
Shape

"Polygons"

Perimeter
Of
Lines
You
Glide
Over
Nonintersecting
Sections

Reflection:
This is a creative and fun way to write in math class and learn. Students can work in groups to compose these and it really enhances the learning as students think about the words and their meanings. One can even get creative with the spelling as shown with the word "Ingulf." It becomes poetry and in math class who would have thought this could occur?

Triangle Personality

Pam Mulson
Elementary Math Coordinator,
Fort Smith Public Schools, Fort Smith, Arkansas

Directions:
Sometimes I use quick writes in math class to assess understanding after a set of lessons. One such quick write directs my students to: *Choose a classification of triangle to describe yourself and tell why it fits your personality.*

Sample of an ELL Student's Response:

"If I would have to choose a triangle or triangles that would fit my personality I would choose a scalene or an obtuse triangle. I chose a scalene triangle because I want my life to be an exciting life with adventures and emotional reasoning. If a life is too balanced it wouldn't be fun would it?

I chose an obtuse triangle because I would like my life to receive all the good stuff it would bring such as good experiences and a successful life as I'm growing up. Both of these triangles fit my personality because I have all the feelings a human being can have and sometimes I can be very open about them but mostly I'm a person that keeps my feelings inside by keeping a straight face expression."

Reflection:
Writing becomes a tool that enables a teacher to know his/her students better. This student reveals so much more than her mathematical understanding in this short prompt. Notice the last sentence, "mostly I'm a person that keeps my feelings inside by keeping a straight face expression." This student reflected mathematical understanding in that a scalene triangle is a triangle where no three sides are congruent. She writes about "balance" and she implies that the scalene triangle is "unbalanced." The obtuse triangle has an obtuse angle (an angle greater than 180 degrees) and she references this in the fact that she is "very open." The writing provides opportunities for teachable moments and helps to generate mathematical discourse between teacher and student and student to student.

VerTEX and PERImeter

Helen Eaton
4th-Grade Teacher,
Holcomb Elementary School, Fayetteville, Arkansas

Directions:
This quick write requires a nice balance between imagination and math vocabulary. Give the following scenario to your students either in written form or orally.

Your friend asked you to take care of his two pets. You know how much he loves them because he talks about Tex and Peri all the time. As he handed you an envelope with instructions about how to take care of them, you asked him how they got their names. He said, "Oh, those are just their nicknames. Their real names are Vertex and Perimeter. Once you've gotten to know them, you'll figure out how they got their names."

Now, write about taking care of your friend's pets and tell what you discovered about them that let you know how they got their names. You may decide what kind of pets they are (fish in a tank, cows in a field, sheep in a barn, dogs in a pen, cats in a house, birds in a cage, iguanas, lizards, ferrets, snakes, and so on).

Remember, in your story, be sure to tell how Tex and Peri got their names.
Give the students 10-12 minutes to write.
Allow students to share part or all of their pieces.

Samples:

I went outside to the horse barn and unlocked the door. There was Peri. She was slowly galloping to the door, but she stayed very close to the barn walls until she stepped out the door. Then I went to the sheep gate. Tex was there in the corner of the pen. He stayed in the corner until I made him come to the gate.

I found out what their names meant easily. I just walked into the shed to find the snake and the fish. The snake was in a square glass box. It was the same length as the edges and was lying in the perfect shape of the glass box. That must have been Perimeter. Then I walked over to the other side of the shed. The fish in the tank had a back fin in the shape of two angles like any fish would. He must be Vertex. That's how I found out which pet had which name.

"Ok, Tex, Peri," I said. "Let's get you two ferrets back into your cage. "Tex! Let go of the corner of the cage! Peri! Why are you running around the perimeter of the room? I'm going to catch you two if I have to set a trap." They must have understood because they both ran into the cage. Tex went to curl up in the corner, and Peri kept running around the sides of the cage. "Ok, now I see. Tex, you like vertexes. Peri, you just like the perimeters."

One day I went to take care of two dogs in separate pens. I was watching them for my friend. I wanted to find out why their names were Vertex and Perimeter. I noticed that Peri kept walking around the edge of his pen, but Tex kept walking from corner to corner.

When I fed them, I noticed that Tex only ate his food out of the corners of his square bowl. Peri ate her food all around the edges of her bowl. She must have been trying to figure out its perimeter.

Reflection:

What a fun quick write this one was! During the quiet writing time, I noticed several times when kids got caught up in their own writing and couldn't help snickering at what they wrote. They did get silly with what they went through in taking care of the pets, but most of them ended up showing somewhere in the piece that they knew the definitions of perimeter and vertex.

I did notice that a couple of students pulled out their math books and flipped to the glossary. I didn't mind that they were getting help with the definitions. I was pleased that they thought to use that resource if they were unsure.

A Diamond Is for Reflecting

Janie Weber
Literacy Coach,
Barling Elementary School, Fort Smith, Arkansas

Directions:

Many mathematic operations are inversions of one another. For example, addition is the opposite of subtraction and multiplication is the inverse of division. It clarifies the students' thinking about these inverse operations to compare and contrast the operations.

The "diamante structure" demands simple comprehension of operations by forcing students to put concepts into a few words. Additionally, the diamante works well with mathematics by offering the opportunity to compare and contrast geometric structures, fractions and decimals, and positive and negative numbers.

Use the ELMO or overhead projector to allow everyone in class to participate in a "Grand Conversation." You may need to review what an *adjective, … ing word,* and *synonym* are—just one more "bang for your buck." Warm up by comparing and contrasting easy ideas such as boys/girls, water/ice, or black/white. After the students are comfortable with the form, the diamante can be used to compare and contrast subject matter content. The following form is my favorite for this writing to learn activity:

Diamante
(noun)
(adjective)   (adjective)
(…ing)   (…ing)   (…ing)
(syn. 1st noun)   (syn. 1st noun.)   (syn. 2nd noun.)   (syn. 2nd noun)
(…ing)   (…ing)   (…ing)
(adjective)   (adjective
(noun)

Reflection:

The diamante poetry form is a terrific method for comparing and contrasting in every subject area. We use it for review across the content area but my first and best experience with it was in leading the children in thinking about multiplication and division. I use this primarily as a whole class activity, although it would be a provocative and valid assessment of learning as well.

Samples by 4th Graders:

Persuasive/Expository Writing

Persuasive
Descriptive, purposeful
Convincing, begging, asking
Letter, e-mail, report, biography
Describing, listing, truth-telling
Realistic, informational
Expository

Rivals

Confederacy
Proud, confident
Seceding, fighting, surrendering
Boys, men, soldiers, survivors
Blockading, defending, emancipating
Determined, noble
Union

Multiplication/Division Diamante

Multiplication
Quick, easy
Adding, Regrouping, Counting
Numbers, Times, Subtract, Numbers
Splitting, Working, Remaining
Mental, math
Division

Number Personalities

Karen Brooks
7th & 8th-Grade Math Teacher,
Ramsey Junior High, Fort Smith, Arkansas

Directions:

This quick write is appropriate for Grades 7 through 12 mathematics classrooms.

Say: *The following excerpt is from Paul Auster's* The Music of Chance, *a novel written in 1990: "I've dealt with numbers all my life, of course, and after a while you begin to feel that each number has a personality of its own. A twelve is very different from a thirteen, for example. Twelve is upright, conscientious, intelligent, whereas thirteen is a loner, a shady character who won't think twice about breaking the law to get what he wants. Eleven is tough, an outdoorsman who likes tramping through woods and scaling mountains; ten is rather simpleminded, a bland figure who always does what he's told; nine is deep and mystical, a Buddha of contemplation ..."*

Have you ever thought about the personalities of numbers? One ... everyone's best friend, Seven ... no one wants to work with him ...

Think of numbers that you like or dislike. Imagine them with personality, hair color, height, and so on. Then, choose just one number and write a description of that number. The description of your number must be detailed enough so that we would recognize him anywhere.

Reflection:

I use this quick write just before I introduce the classifications of numbers in Algebra I (real, rational, irrational, etc.). It has served as a means of getting the students to think of the numbers individually rather than just as groups of numbers. I think it then allows them to examine the definition of classification titles (real, rational, etc.) and gain some insight on why the numbers are classified as they are.

My students enjoy the exercise, and it seems to open the classroom to meaningful discussion.

REFERENCE:

Auster, P. (1990). *The music of chance.* New York: Viking Press.

Polygon Dialogue

Helen Eaton
4th-Grade Teacher,
Holcomb Elementary School, Fayetteville, Arkansas

Directions:

Pass out three trapezoid-shaped pattern blocks to each student. Then allow the students to choose one more pattern block. This fourth block must either be a square or an equilateral triangle. Allow the students to play with the four pattern blocks, arrange them, and then trace them at the top of their papers.

Say: *Think about the blocks in front of you. What makes the trapezoid a trapezoid? Compare the trapezoids to your other polygon? How is it different from either the square of the triangle that you chose? What geometry vocabulary words can help you explain the difference?* As the students name the vocabulary words, list them on the board. Remind them of any important ones that they may have left out. (polygon, vertex, side, angle, obtuse, acute, right angle, equal, parallel, intersecting, etc.) *Now, use your imagination. Pretend that your three trapezoids are a group of friends who go to school together. Pretend that they go to a whole school full of trapezoid-shaped polygons. Then imagine that your other shape, either the square or the triangle, has just moved to their school. Are the trapezoids going to make fun of the different-shaped polygon? Are they going to make friends even though they have differences? How will that square or triangle feel? What will they say to each other? You may give your polygons names and personalities. Use only dialogue as you write. Use the vocabulary words we listed to help you.*

Samples:

The thing said, "Hi, I'm Triangle Lori."
Trapezoid Beth said to Trapezoid Donna, "I don't like her. She only has three vertexes. We have four vertexes."
"I'm supposed to have only three. I'm an equilateral triangle.

"Trapezoid 1 said, "I hate that new thing!"
"Me too. His measurements are weird," said Trapezoid 2.
"Hello, fellow classmates."
"We have more vertexes than you!"
"Polygons, Polygons, What is all this about?"
"They were saying that my vertexes were weird," said the new shape.
"That is not a good reason to fight. I don't even have any vertexes," said Mrs. Circle.

* * *

"Why do you have unequal line segments?" said the square to the trape-zoids.

"That's because we are only allowed to have one set of parallel lines. How do you get to have two sets, Mr. 90 Degrees, with all your equal sides?"

"I'm a square, and I'm proud of it."

"Hi everybody! I'm Square!"

"What are you doing here? Your measurements are way different than ours. We all have some acute angles."

"It's not so bad being different. I like having all right angles."

"Come on. We'll show you around."

Reflection:

My class had been working with polygons in geometry for a while; how-ever, each time they had to name certain polygons they had to think for a minute or they had to guess. I wanted them to do something that would solidify which shape was which. Having the shapes on the paper to hold and manipulate was helpful. This ended up being great fun, but more importantly, we reached the main goal: figuring out what makes a trape-zoid a trapezoid?

This quick write could be used with rhombuses, octagons, hexagons, or any other polygons. It could certainly be adapted to the lower grades by using only squares and triangles.

Can You Build It?

Clare Lesieur
K-4 Academic Coach,
Harrison School District, Harrison, Arkansas

Directions:

Pass out about 20 unifix cubes and an index card to each student. Ask students to create a study carrel by placing books or folders around the perimeter of their desk, so no one can see what they are building. Students should build a simple object using no more than 10 of their unifix cubes. Once they are happy with the object they have built, they should write out the steps to building the object on their index card. The directions should be clear enough that someone could build the object from the directions alone.

Once students are finished, have them exchange cards with a neighbor. Without looking at each other's objects, students should attempt to build their classmate's object following the written directions. Then, students should compare their completed object with their classmate's original object. Do they match? Could they build the object based on the directions? If not, how could the directions be improved upon to make it easier to build the object?

After the first round of the activity, have students revise their initial directions and exchange with a different student. Then ask them to reflect about how their directions improved as a result of their revisions.

Try this same procedure with pattern blocks. Have students create a design and write the directions for building that design. What kind of symmetry does the design have? Can they use the correct names of the shapes rather than just describing them by color?

Reflection:

This is a fun activity that can be done over and over again. Student writing will improve, and the difficulty level can be increased (allow students to use more cubes in their construction or to create more complex patterns).

This quick write can also be done at the conclusion of any art or science project. Ask students to explain the steps in the process by writing a quick how-to paragraph. This is a great way for students to reflect on what they have done. This is also a great connection to practical reading, which often has them follow the steps of a recipe, art project, and so on.

Pattern Block Puzzles

Tina McDonald
2nd-Grade Teacher,
Holcomb Elementary School, Fayetteville, Arkansas

Directions:

- Ask students if they like to put together puzzles.
- Using the overhead the teacher will make a puzzle using 3 pattern block pieces.
- Do not show the puzzle to the students yet.
- Hand out tubs of pattern blocks.

- The teacher gives clues to the students on how to solve the puzzle using pattern blocks.
- The teacher checks individual puzzles for understanding.
- Show the students the correct puzzle arrangement on the overhead.

Explain to the students that they will create their own puzzles with any three pattern blocks. First, they need to build a design with the three pattern blocks. Then, they should copy their design by tracing around the blocks onto the paper. On the next page, they need to write down the directions for building their design so clearly that someone else could build their "puzzle" without seeing the design. Once that is accomplished, the students should trade written directions with a partner. Each student should then attempt to build each other's puzzles by reading and following the written directions.

Reflection:
Students enjoy this quick write activity as they are excited about creating puzzles for the people to solve. What is particularly nice about this activity is that it can be repeated throughout the year by increasing the number of pattern blocks—or using other math objects. Ultimately, the students learn the importance of writing clear and precise directions.

One can also make this activity more germane to mathematics by insisting the students use terms such as hexagon, trapezoid, triangle, rhombus, square, angle, and side.

REFERENCE

Myren, C. (1995) *Posing open-ended questions*. Sacramento, CA: Teaching Resource Center.

SCIENCE AND TECHNOLOGY

Wii-Mote Magic

Shelley Dirst
Literacy Specialist,
Arkansas Department of Education

Directions:

Say: *Listen to this excerpt from an article in the April 28-29, 2007* Wall Street Journal, *titled "Magic Wand: How Hackers Make Use of Their Wii-motes."*

> *A deejay in the Netherlands uses his to mix techno music at dance parties. A medical student in Italy has reprogrammed his to help analyze the results of CT scans. And a Los Angeles software engineer has found a way to get his to help vacuum the floor. The high-tech device in each case: the remote control from a $250 videogame console…. Unlike past remotes, it is motion sensitive and can detect when a player waves it to one side or tilts it forward or back…. The Wii communicates with the on-screen cursor, for example, via an infrared beam. But what has most captivated hackers is a mechanism inside the Wii-mote called an* accelerometer *that can detect its speed and direction of motion… It is the accelerometer … that allows Wii players to use their remotes to act out whatever game they're playing…. The Wii-mote is becoming a cult object for hackers, with gadget geeks re-engineering the device to do all sorts of things having nothing to do with videogames. To repurpose the Wii-mote, they download free software … then tweak that code to assign a specific command to each movement of the device…. Some people are using their remotes to play Laser Tag while others are using them to strum a virtual guitar.*

After allowing some general discussion following this read aloud, I provide the following prompt: Say: *Obviously, Wii makes use of a technology that could have a variety of applications. Devise a new application for the Wii-mote,*

Spark the Brain, Ignite the Pen: Quick Writes for Use in Kindergarten Through High School and Beyond, 2nd Edition, pp. 161–185 *and write a blog entry or letter in which you explain your application to your friends.*

After writing time is over, have students choose the strongest or most interesting point from their response. Allow them to share.

Reflection:

Teachers of all content areas can use the read-aloud practice for a variety of instructional purposes. In this case, an excerpt from a current periodical is used to bring relevant, engaging connections to classroom content. Teachers can select high-interest material from virtually any source to spark discussion, imagination, and even content knowledge about their subject areas.

REFERENCE

Brophy-Warren, J. (2007, April 28-29). Magic wand: How hackers make use of their Wii-motes. *The Wall Street Journal.*

Listen to Your Body

Norma Prentiss
Literacy Coach,
Nelson-Wilks-Herron Elementary, Mountain Home Arkansas

Directions:

Say: *Isn't the human body amazing? All our nerves, muscles, bones and organs work together just right to keep us healthy and safe. I saw a movie once about some scientists who made themselves real tiny and went inside a human body to fight off some germs. I'm going to read a portion of this book about the human body. As I'm reading, think about what it would be like to be a brain. It's like a big computer that controls the rest of your body.*

Read the section of the book, *Inside Your Body,* by Kira Freed, (A-Z reader, level 24) that discusses the muscle system.

After reading that portion of text, say: *Now think about a scary experience, something that made you afraid. Imagine that you are the brain, and your body is sending you messages that you are afraid. What would you tell your body to do? For example:*

Eyes: Uh-oh, I see a big dog coming toward me.

Brain: Okay. Leg muscles start running into the house!

Muscles: You don't have to tell me twice!

Brain: Arm muscles, start pumping. Heart, start beating faster. Mouth, start yelling for help! Lungs, start breathing harder!

Okay, I think we are safe now.

Give student a few minutes to think about a short scenario. Let them write for about ten minutes. Share stories with class.

Reflection:

I got the idea for this quick write from a group of third grade students who, after doing research projects on rain forest animals, wrote a reader's theater script about their animal. Script writing is a great way for students to practice writing dialogue without using quotation marks, which often confuse young writers. Using topics from our science frameworks give students the opportunity to respond to content area topics in a creative way.

It would be helpful to have students brain storm with their partners about their ideas before writing. If they are unfamiliar with reader's theater it might be a good idea to let them work in partners to create their first script. The students will have a great time with this quick write!

How Can the Easter Bunny Lay Eggs?

Helen Eaton
4th-Grade Teacher,
Holcomb Elementary School, Fayetteville, Arkansas

Directions:

After learning about animal classifications, this is a quick write the students will have the background knowledge to enjoy writing and sharing.

Let the students know they'll be doing a quick write so they'll need to get the three necessary materials: pencil, paper, and imagination. It might be helpful for visual learners if they have a copy of the prompt as well as hear it.

Say, *Mammals … Reptiles … Birds … Fish … Marsupials … Amphibians … Insects … Think about all of the different classifications of living things. Each animal fits into a category. But then there's the platypus … Fur like a mammal, lays eggs like a reptile, bill like a bird, webbed feet like an amphibian … It's like the left over pieces got used to make that animal!*

Imagine that you're a scientist who has just discovered an animal that's never been seen before. You're amazed because it doesn't fit into an animal classification. Describe your animal. Where did you find it? What does it look like? What traits does it have? What does it eat? How does it care for its young? What covers its body? How does it move?

Your animal must have traits from at least two classifications. (Sorry, you can't choose human and spider. Someone already wrote that movie script.)

Have the kids daydream for 1 to 2 minutes to imagine their animal before writing. Give ten minutes to write, then allow students to share.

Reflection:

The idea for this quick write came about after one of my students jokingly asked, "How does the Easter Bunny lay eggs?" We'd been learning about animal classification, and I thought this would be a fun way for the kids to show what they'd learned about the different types of animals.

They were ready to start writing immediately after I'd read the quick write directions, but I made them wait two minutes before I let them put pencil to paper so that they could get a clear picture of their new animal. They wrote fast and long and couldn't wait to share.

My intention was that they write about the traits they saw in their new animal that would cause it to be classified in various ways; however, I don't think I stressed that aspect enough. Their pieces were more about the mixing of specific animals. There was a feathered fish that could fly out of the water, a catfish with a furry tail and pointed ears that purred, and a "lish" which was a lizard fish that could swim like a fish and crawl like a lizard. There was a bullfrog that was a furry amphibian that mooed in the evenings, a turtle hawk that could only fly low because its shell was too heavy to fly high, and a chicken with gills so it could dive for its food at the bottom of the lake. I especially liked the scaly frog that hatched eggs in its pouch then nursed the young when they hatched. (That one included nearly all the animal classifications!) They loved writing about themselves as "Professor Smith" or as "Dr. Jones" and referring to themselves as scientists or explorers. Their stories gave lots of details about where they were when the new animal was discovered and what happened when they tried to catch it. If my intent had been to truly assess their knowledge about animal classifications, then I might have wanted a do-over. But, one never knows quite how the brains will be sparked with a quick write, and since the pens were ignited, I felt like it was a successful use of time.

Creating the World Anew

Samuel Totten
*Founder and Director of the Northwest Arkansas Writing Project
and Professor of Curriculum and Instruction,
University of Arkansas, Fayetteville*

Directions:

Over the past 70 years advances in the areas of science and technology have been nothing short of phenomenal. For many decades into the twentieth century (in some cases up through the 1980s), average members of society did not have wide access to a wide range of items that we accept as givens in today's world, including but not limited to the following: television (let alone colored TV sets or flat screen TVs), desktop computers, air conditioning in homes, DVDs, iPods, fax machines, video cameras, supersonic jets, Xerox machines, text-messaging, home printers, and so on.

Take several minutes and list those items that you consider most revolutionary in today's world. That done, take 5 minutes and write about the one item you either could not live without and why or the one item you could live without, if you had to, and why.

Reflection:

This simple activity, which is ideal for science/technology, history and English courses, helps students appreciate the astonishing advancement of science and technology, the amazing world in which they live, and the many and varied tools they have at their disposal which people in the past didn't have but that we now, largely, take for granted.

Creature Features

Clare Lesieur
K-4 Academic Coach,
Harrison School District, Harrison, Arkansas

Directions:
Read *Creature Features* by David Drew. In this book, students are asked to guess what is "in the box" by solving riddles that describe different animals. For example, the following description is given:

How many legs? Eight
How many eyes? Eight
What's its color? Black
What's its shape? Round
What does it feel like? Hairy
It must be a … spider.

After solving the riddles in the book, have the class brainstorm animals they know about. Record on chart paper. Then, create a riddle whole-class and display as a model. Ask students to write their own riddles to share with the class. Students can use the class list or come up with their own ideas. They can write question/answers or a list of sentences to provide the clues. Remind the students to give enough information so their classmates can solve the riddle. Be sure to allow for plenty of share time, as everyone will want to share!

Reflection:
Students love writing and guessing riddles! This is a great way to teach inferences, speaking/listening skills, and connect reading and writing to science. With younger kids, I usually let them start off writing riddles in small groups. You may consider providing a riddle template like the one below, especially when working with kindergarten students:

How many legs? _____
How many eyes? _____
What's its color? _____
What's its shape? _____
What does it feel like? _____
It must be a _____.

Riddles can be used with any topic that students know well. I have used them with fairy tale characters, geometric shapes, and occupations. Students enjoy making riddle books and placing them in the class library.

I have used this particular lesson with older students as well as primary students. After writing research papers on insects, my fourth graders wrote riddles to share their information with the class. Although we were unable to guess many of the specific insects, we learned a lot about a variety of interesting bugs.

Creature Features is currently out of print, but many primary teachers have it in big book form. If you do not have access to the book, you can create your own riddles to share with the class prior to the lesson. For extra fun, bring in a shoebox with holes punched in the top. Whoever is sharing their riddle can hold the box and say, "In this box, I have a creature. Can you guess what it is?" and then share their riddle. This is sure to motivate your kids!

REFERENCE

Drew, D. (1988). *Creature features*. Black Heath, New South Wales, Australia: Black Cockatoo.

Here We Go 'Round ...

Helen Eaton
4th-Grade Teacher,
Holcomb Elementary School, Fayetteville, Arkansas

Directions:

Display an assortment of items that represent a cycle that occurs in nature. (Seeds, flowers, and fruit might represent the life cycle. Pieces of lava, limestone, and marble might represent the rock cycle. Ice, water, and a spray bottle might represent the water cycle.) Also make available a diagram which includes vocabulary important to the content of the particular cycle.

If this is done as schema activation for a new unit of study, have enough of the items so that students can have a hands-on experience with each one. They'll need to touch, hold, smell, squish, or squirt each item. The diagram and vocabulary will need to be big enough for all to see from their seats or on individual handouts.

If this is done as at the end of a unit of study, the items may simply serve as concrete reminders of the content that has been covered.Placing them at the front of the room or on tables near the students may be sufficient.The diagram and vocabulary may already be in their student learning logs, notes, or memories.

After the students have had time for observation, ask them to close their eyes. *Picture one of the items from the cycle. Try to imagine that it had a personality. Try to imagine that it had feelings and thoughts. Try to imagine yourself as that item. What have you been through? How have you changed as you've passed through each stage of your cycle? What forms have you taken? Where have you been? How long were you in each stage? What made you leave each stage? Which stage was the best? Which was the worst? Why? Which stage do you think you'll go through next?*

Now, think about telling your story. You might start by writing something like, "I may look like fresh clean water right now, but let me tell you what I've been through to get in this glass…" As you tell your story, be sure to include each step of the cycle using the vocabulary that will explain what you've been through and what you are, as well as what you have been.

Give the students ten minutes to write, and then allow them to share their cycle experiences.

Reflection:

I have used versions of this quick write in several ways. It has been most successful when done near the end of a unit. After the content has been taught, this gives students an opportunity to expand their new knowledge in a different and creative way. There might be this from a glass of water: "I was having a perfectly fine time as a raindrop dancing in the cloud with my buddies when I got too heavy and fell out. I was so scared when I was falling. Landing in the ocean didn't hurt, but it tasted awful. I couldn't wait to evaporate and get back into the sky.…" Or this from a piece of lava: "I must have been in that magma chamber for a thousand years before it was finally my turn to spew right out onto the surface. I wanted to stay that way for a while. I'd been crunched into sediments a million years before and that wasn't all it was cracked up (get it?) to be …"Most didn't want to stop writing until they'd "visited" each stage of their chosen cycle.

During a workshop for teachers, I set up a center for the life cycle, the rock cycle, and another for the water cycle. Because they had background knowledge for each of the cycles, they were allowed to choose which they would "become part of." Like the kids, they didn't want to stop until they'd "proven" that they knew the stages of the cycle in their stories.

Shark or Dolphin? You Decide

Shannon Boyd
Middle School Teacher,
Kirksey Middle School, Rogers, Arkansas

Directions:

Often, science seems obscure and abstract. Actually, concepts in this subject area can be more readily remembered if students are able to make a personal connection.

After reading *All About Ocean Animals*, or *Ocean Animals*, give students time to brainstorm qualities of ocean mammals and ocean fish.

Using a graphic organizer, give students time to discuss facts about mammals and fish that live in the ocean.

Now, have students compare themselves/their family to either mammals or fish, by completing the statement, "I belong to a family of _____." Students will then write to explain why they decided on their choice. Prompt students, if necessary, by asking them questions such as:

- Do you have many family members?
- Do your parents spend a lot of time with you?
- Do you have to "fend for yourself," or do you have someone to guide you?

Provide opportunities for students to share.

Reflection:

Depending on the trust level within the classroom, students may/may not be willing to share. You can, however, gain valuable insight not only into your students' understanding of the information, but also their perception of their "place" within their family structure from this exercise.

REFERENCES

Evert, L., Vogel, J., Feeney, K., & Corrigan, P. (2001). *Ocean animals.* New York: Northwood Press.

Somerville, L. (2007). *All about ocean animals.* New York: Silver Dolphin Books.

What the World Be Like Without ...

Samuel Totten
Founder and Director of the Northwest Arkansas Writing Project
and Professor of Curriculum and Instruction,
University of Arkansas, Fayetteville

Direction:

Most individuals (children and adults alike) have a tendency to accept life as it is at face value. That is, many, if not most, rarely contemplate how the world would be a vastly different place if specific discoveries had not been made, inventions had not been created and/or various items (e.g., cars, email, the internet, running water, cooling and heating in homes) were not readily available.

Ask students to brainstorm those discoveries, inventions, items that they consider "a common everyday occurrence in society" that are, in fact, really rather remarkable both when one thinks about it and one considers what life would be like without them. As a starter, a teacher may wish to list four or five of his/her own examples: automobile, Xerox machine, computer, Internet, and so on.

Once the list has been completed and written on the board or over-head, the students should be asked to pick one item on the list and discuss both how they, in fact, either take it for granted and/or how vastly different their life would be did it not exist.

Reflection:

This quick write helps students to reflect on their world, the technology they use, and how technology assists them to live their daily lives. It also, hopefully, opens their eyes to the remarkable world of inventions.

Take a Haiku Hike!

Clare Lesieur
K-4 Academic Coach,
Harrison School District, Harrison, Arkansas

Directions:

This lesson is adapted from the book, *Haiku Hike*, written and illustrated by fourth grade students from St. Mary's Catholic School in Mansfield, Massachusetts. Read the book to your class. Discuss how the authors used haiku as a way to capture the nature scenes from their hike.Review sensory details and discuss how adding sensory details to our writing helps us paint a picture for our readers.

Now you are ready for your hike! Take students to the playground, a park or nature trail, or an outdoor classroom. You can even watch a nature video or visualize a nature scene if taking an actual hike is not an option. Ask students to record impressions or observations as they participate in their "hike." These can be written as words or phrases: red, orange, brown leaves, black bird hopping, cool wind blowing my hair, crunch of dried leaves, bright blue sky, and so on.

After the hike, return to the classroom and discuss the elements of haiku. Revisit some of the examples from *Haiku Hike*. Challenge students to reword their phrases to match the model (using correct syllables).For example:

Happy blackbird hops
On brittle leaves, brown and red
Under bright blue skies

Reflection:

The haiku format can be challenging, especially for younger students. Other poetry forms can be used. Kindergarten students especially enjoy writing list poems.

It is important that students are quiet and focused during their hike in order to fully experience the setting and record their observations. My students always take this seriously, often venturing off on their own to write and reflect. I also encourage students to sketch in their journals. Nature journaling is a great way to combine writing, science, and art.

After writing our haikus, we type them on the computer and illustrate with crayon or watercolor. These make nice class books or can be mounted on construction paper and displayed in the hall. This is also a great project to use with digital cameras. Be imaginative!

REFERENCE

Students of St. Mary's Catholic School. (2005) *Haiku hike.* New York: Scholastic.

Nature's Treasures

Clare Lesieur
4th-Grade Teacher,
Skyline Heights Elementary School, Harrison, Arkansas

Directions:

Before providing the actual directions, I should provide some background information for the reader: "Nature Journaling" is a combination of art, reading, writing, and science. The purpose is to have students explore the world around them through inquiry-based nature study and record their discoveries through art, poetry, and narrative and descriptive writing. Many nature journaling activities take place outdoors. This activity, however, is perfect for that time when you wish to bring the outdoors in.

You will need a collection of interesting items from nature (rocks, shells, nests, etc.). Place these in one or more baskets. Also include an envelope with copies of "observation poems" to serve as examples. Allow students to observe the objects and select one or more items to sketch in their journals. As they are sketching, ask them to write down their thoughts, observations, and/or connections related to the object.

Suggest one or more of the following possibilities to the students:

1. *The item you are sketching may remind you of a place you once visited or of a time when something interesting happened to you. Make your own connection and write about it.*

2. *Think about the item as you are sketching. Where did it come from? How does it fit into the natural world? Write a story about it. (For example, using the bird's nest, write about the baby birds that once lived there.)*

3. *Write an observation poem about your object. First, though, read the observation poems in the basket for inspiration.*

Reflection:

My students have brought in many of the items in my basket. We keep the objects in our classroom in a "touch box." Children are fascinated by the natural world, and nature journaling, both in and outside of the class-room, provides endless inspiration for writing.

And Just Who's to Blame?

Amy Young
Literacy Specialist,
OUR Educational Cooperative, Harrison, Arkansas

Directions:

To get students to consider just who is to blame for the "obesity epi-demic" in the United States today, read aloud the following excerpt from the article "Super-sized Nation: Are fast-food restaurants responsible for teens' obesity?" which appeared in the March 7, 2003 edition of Scholastic *Scope* student magazine: (Before reading the selection, explain to students that a group of New York teens filed a lawsuit against McDonald's in the fall of 2002 claiming that the Golden Arches had helped create a nation of obesity. Ask students to evaluate the evidence. Do they think the stu-dents had a case?)

"Fatty Foods"

"'We are in the middle of an epidemic of obesity, which starts in childhood," says Richard Daynard, a law professor at Northeastern University. Fast-food restaurants contribute to the problem, he says.

Supporters of the suit, like Daynard, say that fast-food restaurants should let customers know how many calories are in each meal. "If people were told, a lot of people would order smaller sizes or order something else," says Daynard.

Critics also say that quick-service chains should stop pitching "super-sized" packages that are loaded with calories—typically more than half of what the government recommends for a day. What's worse, Daynard says, is that fast-food chains market to very young kids, who are easily influenced.

"Personal Choices"

"Obesity does not come down to one simple problem," says Sheila Cohn, manager of nutrition policy at the National Restaurant Association. "Chil-dren aren't as active as they used to be. That's a huge part of it.'

Cohn and other opponents of the suit say that restaurants are only responsible for providing food, not for what people choose to eat or how much. "These lawsuits are taking all of your personal responsibility and throwing it away," Cohn says. Critics of the suit also note that fast-food restaurants do offer healthy choices.

Ask students what they think. Are fast-food chains responsible for teens' obesity? Or does each individual have the responsibility of monitoring what goes into his body? Students need to provide support for their opinions.

Allow 10 minutes for students to respond to the prompt. Encourage students to share their opinions and discuss their ideas.

Reflection:

This quick write activity provides a lively introduction to a nutrition study in a health or consumer science class. It could also be used as one concludes the unit, emphasizing the importance of each person taking responsibility for his own health.

REFERENCE

Holliday, H. (2003, March 7). Supersized nation: Are fast-food restaurants responsible for teens' obesity? *Scope, 51*(14).

Take a Ride on the Magic School Bus

Clare Lesieur
4th-Grade Teacher,
Skyline Heights Elementary School, Harrison, Arkansas

Directions:

Most primary and intermediate-level students are familiar with *The Magic School Bus* series. Whether traveling inside the human body or inside the Earth or out to space, students learn science concepts while enjoying an animated adventure. Show a clip of a *Magic School Bus* video or read a selection from one of the books. (For a complete listing, go to the official Scholastic Web site at www.scholastic.com/magicschoolbus/home_2.htm.)

Then inform the students of the following: *Your task is to pretend you are a character on the Magic School Bus. How would you explore [assigned topic]? Write a paragraph describing your travels. You must include at least three [or any assigned number] important and accurate facts. You may refer to your science book if needed to verify information.*

Give students about 10 minutes to work on their stories, and then allow time to share.

Reflection:

This is a great way to assess student learning at the end of a science unit. The quick write can be extended from a paragraph to a full story. This is always a favorite with my kids and a great cross-curricular activity!

Seeing Through the Eyes of Another

Mary Wince
Literacy Coach,
Bruno-Pyatt School, Eros, Arkansas

Directions:

Encourage your students to summarize nonfiction text by writing from a novel point of view. Author Diane Siebert does just this in her picture book *Mojave*. She reveals the mysteries of the desert by writing from the viewpoint of the Mojave. Her book begins with the lines: *"I am the desert.I am free. Come walk the sweeping face of me."*

Begin the quick write with the following directions: *As I read the book* Mojave, *listen for the ways in which author Diane Siebert uses sensory details to describe the desert. Notice the way she celebrates the landscape of the desert by writing in the voice of the desert itself. How does she do this? Think about it as I read.*

After sharing the book, ask the students to recall several sensory details used to describe the desert.Briefly discuss how the author writes from the first person point of view by using *I am ..., I feel ..., I hear ....* Then use the following prompt: *Now it's your turn. Think about a habitat we have been studying about in science. Use sensory details to describe the habitat. Try to write from the viewpoint of the habitat itself.* After a brief time to write, invite several students to share.

Reflection:

Inspired by this quick write, students in Grades 2-6 wrote with ease from the first person viewpoint of a habitat. As an alternative to Siebert's *Mojave,* consider sharing *I Am the Mummy Heb-Nefert* by Eve Bunting or *If A Bus Could Talk: The Story of Rosa Parks* by Faith Ringgold as a stimulus for the quick write. Both are written from the first person point of view. This quick write is easily adapted to encourage students to write first person accounts from the viewpoint of animals or historical figures. I've included two animal samples below. The student samples represent polished writing. During a field trip to the nearby Buffalo River, fifth and sixth graders did a bit of nature journaling and captured sensory details in writers' notebooks. They transformed their notes into first person accounts, read their writing orally, played with line order and word choice, received feedback from response groups and revised. Younger students revisited informational text to collect additional details about planets and animals and then revised their initial writing.

Samples of Student Writing from 5th & 6th Graders:

The Buffalo River

I am the Buffalo River
I am free
Hear the hush and whistle of me
Come swim in the calming current of me.
Come float the rushing waters of me
I am the Buffalo River
I am free
See the painted turtles of me
Sunning themselves on my smooth boulders
While the red-tailed hawk circles my shoulders

Through the gentle season of spring
And the simmering season of summer
Through the bold season of autumn leaves
And the shivering season of bare trees
Through wind and rain, snow or shine
I am the Buffalo River
I am free

The Ozark Mountains

I am the Ozark Mountains
Noble with age
Come walk the peaks and valleys of me
Years and years of wind and rain
Have worn me smooth
My rocky face is shaded with oaks and pines
And fragile dogwoods dot my sides

I am the Ozark Mountains
A shelter free
Animals make their homes in me

I feel the hooves of white-tailed deer
And the paws of coyotes pad over me
The cry of the hawk, the raucous crow
Echo in my mountaintop ears

I am the Ozark Mountains
A bird's eye view
I see the river weave for miles below
The small-mouth bass glimmer and shine
The turtle snaps at dragonflies
A kingfisher dips for a midday meal
I watch in peace from my perch so high

I am the Ozark Mountains
So noble with age

Samples of Student Writing from 2nd & 3rd Graders:

The Moon

I am the moon.
You can see me from your home.
I circle around the Earth in 28 days.
I am not a planet.
I am a satellite.
I am part of the solar system.
You can only visit me by flying in a spacecraft.
A long time ago, the astronaut Neil Armstrong stepped on me.
He left his footprint.
He had to wear a space suit because I am very cold in the shade and very hot in the sun.
He had to wear a backpack with air to breathe.
I can still see his footprint because there is no wind on me to blow it away.
I am the moon.

Venus

I am Venus.
I am the second planet in the solar system.
I orbit around the Sun.
I am called Earth's sister because we are almost the same size.
We both have clouds.
We both are made out of rock and metal.
But I am closer to the Sun than Earth.
It is hotter on me than on Earth.
The clouds on Earth are made of water.
But some of my clouds are made of acid that would burn your skin.
Almost all of me is covered with melted rock and metal called lava.
Nothing can live in lava.

So you cannot visit me.
I am Venus.

Tiger Shark

I am the tiger shark.
I have black stripes on my back and a white belly.
I have sharp serrated teeth like a saw.
When one of my teeth falls out, another one will grow in its place.
What do you think about that?
My long tail helps me swim fast in the ocean when I search for food.
I am not a picky eater!
Sometimes I hunt live animals, but other times I eat carrion—dead and rotting animals.
I am a great junk eater, too.
In fact, I am nicknamed the *trash can of the sea* because sometimes I swallow junk like glass bottles and clothes.
I am the tiger shark.

Tasmanian Devil

I am the Tasmanian devil.
You can find me in Tasmania, an island near Australia.
I am a scavenger.
I am nocturnal.
I sleep during the day and look for food at night.
Sometimes I use my sharp teeth to kill small animals, but usually I eat the dead, rotting bodies of animals.
I am about the size of a small dog.
I have black fur with white on my back and chest.
I am a marsupial.
When I was a baby, I grew in my mother's pouch.
When you see my pink ears turn purple, stay away!
That means I am really angry!
Watch out for me!
I am the Tasmanian devil.

REFERENCES

Bunting, E. (1997). *I am the mummy Heb-Nefert.* Orlando, FL: Harcourt.
Ringgold, F. (1999). *If a bus could talk: The story of Rosa Parks.* New York: Scholastic.
Siebert, D. (1988). *Mojave.* New York: Harper Trophy.

Tell Me What's So Important

Mary Wince
Literacy Coach,
Bruno-Pyatt School, Eros, Arkansas

Directions:

This quick write is designed to help students determine what's important when writing information. Author Margaret Wise Brown demonstrates this strategy in *The Important Book.* Here's an excerpt: "*The important thing about a spoon is that you eat with it. It's like a little shovel. You hold it in your hand. You can put it in your mouth.… But the most important thing about a spoon is that you eat with it.… The important thing about rain is that it is wet. It falls out of the sky, and it sounds like rain, and it makes things shiny.… But the important thing about rain is that it is wet.*"

Begin by sharing several pages from *The Important Book* by Margaret Wise Brown. Then instruct students to think about a non-fiction topic they are currently exploring in an informational text, possibly in science, social studies, or reading class. After reading, share the following prompt: *In* The Important Book, *author Margaret Wise Brown captures what is important about each object she describes and then adds details. Think about a topic you are learning about.* (Here you can specify a topic.) *Try your hand at writing what's important about your topic. Don't forget to add some details.* After a brief time to write, invite several students to share.Students who have not had an opportunity to share with the entire group may turn to someone sitting near them to share.

Reflection:

I have used this quick write with success in grades K-3. To elevate the quality of writing of young students, we briefly discuss the author's craft. Students easily identify the pattern: *The important thing about* _____ *is* _____, followed by additional details and concluding with *But the important thing about* _____ *is* _____. Together we brainstorm facts we have learned about a topic and discuss one we think is most important. Since students often have difficulty choosing the most important fact, I model using an explicit think aloud. After working as a large group, students in second and third grade work in small groups or individually to compose additional writing pieces. As an added bonus, after using this format students are readily able to transform *the important thing* into a topic sentence.

Samples of Group Nonfiction Writing From 2nd & 3rd Graders:

A Chick

The important thing about a chick is that it is a bird and hatches from an egg.
It grows from an embryo inside an egg.
It is ready to hatch in 21 days.
At first a chick is wet and ugly.
It is covered with feathers called down.
The down dries really fast
Then the chick is fluffy and cute.
A chick grows more feathers.
It grows a comb and a wattle.
A chick might grow up to be a boy chicken called a rooster.
It might grow up to be a girl chicken called a hen.
But the important thing about a chick is that it is a bird and hatches from an egg.

A Tadpole

The important thing about a tadpole is that it grows into a frog or a toad.
It looks like a fish, but it is not a fish.
A tadpole is an amphibian.
It lives in the water and on the land.
A tadpole hatches from an egg.
It has gills to help get air from the water.
It eats algae in the water.
Then the tadpole gets bigger.
It grows back legs.
It loses its tail and grows front legs.
It grows lungs to breathe air.
It can jump out of the water onto the land.
It might grow into a frog with smooth skin.
It might grow into a toad with bumpy skin.
But the important thing about a tadpole is that it grows into a frog or a toad.

Jane Goodall

The important thing about Jane Goodall is that she loves learning about animals.
She worked at a park in Tanzania, Africa.
She studied chimpanzees for many years.
Jane's first chimp friend was David Greybeard.
She learned that chimps use sticks to get termites to eat.
She learned that when chimps talk to each other they hoot and grunt and bark.

She learned that sometimes chimps hug and kiss and sometimes they are sad.
She opened an orphanage for baby chimps with no mothers.
But the important thing about Jane Goodall is that she loves learning about animals.

A Scavenger

The important thing about a scavenger is that it helps prevent the spread of disease.
It eats dead and rotting bodies of other animals called carrion.
A scavenger might also be a junk eater that eats garbage left by humans.
It might be a bird like the vulture or the raven.
It might be a mammal like the striped hyena.
It might be an amphibian like the African clawed frog or a fish like the tiger shark.
It might be even be a marsupial like the Tasmanian devil.
A scavenger might be endangered like the California condor.
But the important thing about a scavenger is that it helps prevent the spread of disease.

Sample of Group Fiction Writing from 3rd Graders:

Charlotte

The important thing about Charlotte is that she saves Wilbur's life.
She lives in a barn on Zuckerman's farm.
She is a friend to all the animals.
She keeps an eye out for Templeton.
Charlotte knows how to solve problems.
She is a great reader and writer.
She weaves special webs.
She has lots and lots of babies.
But the important thing about Charlotte is that she saves Wilbur's life.

REFERENCE

Brown, M. (1949/1977). *The important book*. Cincinnati, OH: HarperTrophy

What Makes a Human Being Human?

Samuel Totten
*Founder and Director of the Northwest Arkansas Writing Project
and Professor of Curriculum and Instruction,
University of Arkansas, Fayetteville*

Directions:

The teacher should ask and relate the following to the students: "*Have you ever stopped to consider or ponder about what makes a human being 'human'? That is, have you ever thought seriously about what makes human beings such a unique species? Over the past several years many philosophers, theologians and other scholars have pondered this issue and have come up with some very provocative thoughts/insights. Among some of the many, for example, are that humans can think about their thoughts (metacognition); humans created and use language; humans have ethical systems; humans experience self-awareness; humans believe in and practice religion.*

I want you to take a few minutes and list as many ideas you have in regard to the question, "What makes a human being 'human'?" Once you've come up with at least a half dozen or so, I want you to write a short piece in which you tie together those ideas that you think get to the crux of the matter. It can take any form you wish and be serious or humorous.

Reflection:

This has proved to be an incredibly interesting quick write that truly results in a lot of student thought and wrestling with who and what they are as a species. This is an excellent quick write for use in the science classroom, from general science to biology.

What's Next? Extinguishing Our World?

Samuel Totten
*Founder and Director of the Northwest Arkansas Writing Project
and Professor of Curriculum and Instruction,
University of Arkansas, Fayetteville*

Directions:

The teacher should say: *The United Nations recently reported that earth faces "the worst spate of extinctions since the dinosaurs vanished 65 million years ago, with man-made threats such as rising populations, felling of forests, hunting, pollution and climate change." That is a profoundly disturbing fact, and one that not only impacts the animals (and plants) that are being lost today, but humanity living both today and all of the future.*

Next, the teacher should read the article, "Scientists Fear Wave of Animal Extinction," from *The St. Petersburg Times* (November 7, 2008) to his/her students.

Scientists Fear Wave of Animal Extinctions
Alister Doyle
Reuters

OSLO—The Yangtze River dolphin, the Christmas Island shrew and the Venezuelan skunk frog are all victims in an alarming flood of extinctions, but how do scientists decide when such "possibly extinct" creatures no longer exist?

The United Nations says the world faces the worst spate of extinctions since the dinosaurs vanished 65 million years ago, with man-made threats such as rising populations, felling of forests, hunting, pollution and climate change.

Yet proving that any individual species has gone the way of the dodo necessarily demands long, fruitless searching.

"If there's one thing in my career I'd like to be proved wrong about, it's the baiji," said Sam Turvey of the Zoological Society of London, using another name for the Yangtze River dolphin.

Turvey spent almost 3 months this year interviewing Chinese fishermen in vain for sightings of the long-snouted dolphin, which has not been seen since 2002. Some colleagues in China are still looking.

The baiji was almost declared extinct in 2006 after an acoustic and visual survey of the river turned up nothing. Then, a blurry video gave experts pause, and it was rated "possibly extinct."

About 300 plant and animal species, including the Christmas Island shrew and the Venezuelan skunk frog are also "possibly extinct," the worst category short of extinction, according to the International Union for Conservation of Nature's (IUCN) Red List.

If Turvey's study turns up no firm evidence, it will likely push the Yangtze River dolphin into the "extinct" column, said Mike Hoffmann, who manages a global project to assess species for the IUCN and Conservation International.

It would be the first "megafauna" mammal—one weighing more than 100 kilograms—to die out since the Caribbean monk seal in the 1950s.

Scientists working on the "possibly extinct" list rummage in the undergrowth for rare plants, frogs or rats, set up night-time traps for bats or moths, or scour the seabed for corals.

Some experts liken the difficulties to "proving" that the mythical Loch Ness Monster does not exist.

The Christmas Island shrew has not been seen on its Australian island since 1985. The Venezuelan skunk frog, known from a cloud forest habitat of 10 square kilometers, has not been spotted despite repeated searches.

Despite the difficulties of proof, scientists say species are disappearing at an ever faster rate.

Some 76 mammals have gone extinct since 1500, a much faster rate than in previous centuries, and 29 are "possibly extinct" on the 2008 Red List.

BACK FROM THE DEAD

Extinct species have often unknown economic value, such as the Australian gastric brooding frog, which incubated its young in its stomach and might have pointed to ways to treat ulcers. Or South Africa's bluebuck antelope, which could have boosted tourism.

And, when one species goes extinct, new ones become endangered, as is happening on the Yangtze River, where the finless porpoise and the Chinese paddlefish, reported to grow up to 7 meters, are also in danger.

"The problem with the Yangtze is that the threats are still there and they are escalating," Turvey said.

And there are wider threats. The UN Climate Panel said in 2007 that up to 30 percent of species will face increasing risks of extinction if temperatures rise by another 1 degree Celsius.

The panel, which says temperatures rose 0.7 C in the 20th century, also forecasts more droughts, heatwaves and rising seas linked to human emissions of greenhouse gases spurred mainly by burning fossil fuels.

In a 2006 report, Birdlife expert Stuart Butchart wrote that 150 bird species had gone extinct since 1500, or 0.3 a year. That was 30-300 times the background rate of extinctions—a natural process deduced from fossil records.

No one knows the number of species on earth—one UN-backed study estimated 5-30 million against about 2 million documented so far. The UN Convention on Biological Diversity estimates they may be vanishing faster than they are found, at a rate of three per hour, the fastest in millions of years.

Next say: *While this article mentioned some of the detrimental impacts of the extinction of plants and animals, it only touched on the issue. Over and above the loss of a part of our world, one of the most harmful impacts of the extinction of plants and animals is that such extinction actually poses real and incredible threat to humanity's continued existence. This is understood more clearly when one realizes that human beings currently use some 40,000 different plant, animal, fungi, bacteria and virus species for food, pharmaceutical products, industrial products. Researchers also believe that plants that have yet to be discovered in jungles in South America, for example, have the possibility of being used for some of the gravest diseases facing humanity, including cancer.*

Next: *Ask the students to write a short response (in which he/she agrees or disagrees) with the following assertion which shall be used for reflective and discussion purposes: "Extinction is a problem for scientists to worry about, not average human beings."*

Reflection:

Each time an animal or plant is extinguished the world loses something it will never gain back. That loss is permanent, forever. That is a striking and profound matter, but very few individuals, other than scientists (such as biologists, botanists, ethnobotanists) and conservationists seem to care about such a phenomenon. This quick write, hopefully, will wake students up to the issue of extinction and what it means for our world.

REFERENCE

Doyle, A. (2008, November 7). Scientists fear wave of animal extinction. *The St. Petersburg Times*. Retrieved from http://www.sptimes.ru/index.php%3Fstory_id%3D27557%26action_id

SOCIAL STUDIES

Looking the Other Way:
What's It Take to Be
Our Brothers' and Sisters' Keeper?

Samuel Totten
*Founder and Director of the Northwest Arkansas Writing Project
and Professor of Curriculum and Instruction,
University of Arkansas, Fayetteville*

Directions:

For an introduction to the issue of the concept/phenomena of "bystanders" during the Holocaust (or any other genocide for that matter), tell or read the students the story of Kitty Genovese being attacked. (Teachers can obtain an online article about the plight and fate of this young New York woman by Googling: The Killing of Kitty Genovese + Michael Dorman.) Read up to the point where she is crying for help the second time. Then have the students respond in writing in regard to what they think the various individuals actually did who heard her pleas. After having various students share their pieces/thoughts, read the rest of the news story about what actually took pace.

A variation of this activity could have the students write out what they would have done and why. Then, once the rest of the story is read, a short class discussion could ensue.

Spark the Brain, Ignite the Pen: Quick Writes for Use in Kindergarten Through High School and Beyond, 2nd Edition, pp. 189–219

Reflection:
This quick write helps students to understand the complexity of the so-called "bystander syndrome" as well as social and personal responsibility. It always results in heated and thought-provoking class discussion.

This quick write is also powerful for use in English, composition and speech classes. Creative teachers will find that it can be used with different pieces of literature, various writing assignments, and different kinds of speeches.

"I'll Never Forget Where I Was When ..."

Samuel Totten
*Founder and Director of the Northwest Arkansas Writing Project
and Professor of Curriculum and Instruction,
University of Arkansas, Fayetteville*

Directions:
Each generation, it seems, experiences something so shocking, so out of the ordinary, so astonishing, so unbelievable, so unimaginable that when such an incident or event is referred to, individuals often begin their sentences with one of these two phrases: "I'll never forget where I was when ..." or "I'll never forget what I was doing when ..."

Over the past 80 years, the incidents/events that have been referred to in such ways are, for example: the Japanese bombing of Pearl Harbor (December 7, 1941); the atomic bombing of Hiroshima by the United States (August 6, 1945); the assassination of President John F. Kennedy by Lee Harvey Oswald (November 22, 1963); the assassination of Martin Luther King Jr. by James Earl Ray (April 4, 1968); Neil Armstrong's first step on the moon (July 20, 1969); and the terrorist attack and destruction of the Twin Towers in New York City (September 11, 2001).

Please take 5 minutes and write a short response to the terrorist attack on 9/11. In doing so, use one of the aforementioned phrases as a first line: "I'll never forget where I was when ..." or "I'll never forget what I was doing when ..." (Note: If a teacher feels he/she must provide some examples of what he/she is referring to, then it is advisable to provide examples from earlier periods of time—prior to when the students were born. That way students are not inclined to simply use an example that the teacher has given.)

Reflection:
This is a remarkably powerful quick write for students of all ages—elementary through the university level. It is a quick write that encourages students to reflect on how history is made, impacts people, and is not something ancient but alive.

Capturing Personal, Local, National, and International History in a Time Capsule

Samuel Totten
*Founder and Director of the Northwest Arkansas Writing Project
and Professor of Curriculum and Instruction,
University of Arkansas, Fayetteville*

Directions:
The teacher should tell the students the following: *Local communities, schools and various organizations have created time capsules in order to provide information to people 100 years in the future about life as it was 100 years earlier. They also do so as a way of celebrating and commemorating the history and lives within the community in which they reside or organizations to which they belong. It is also an enjoyable way to focus attention on the significance of local history and lore.*

In the next few minutes, please give serious thought to those items—at least 10—that you personally think should be included in a time capsule of your life on earth thus far. In doing so, remember that the items must easily fit into a capsule no more than three feet long and a foot in diameter. In coming up with your ideas try to include at least one item in each of these categories (an overhead of items to be shown on an overhead): a recording of a TV show or movie; a recording of a song; a book; an article about a famous event; biography of a famous person who you think is particularly interesting; a unique toy or game; a photo essay on or about a highly significant event that took place somewhere in the world during your lifetime; the name and description of an invention during your lifetime that you think is exciting, valuable, important or just plain "cool"; a piece of art; a description of a major discovery; an article about an infamous person; an article about an infamous event. You may, of course, include anything else you wish. In selecting items, be sure that they are truly illustrative of your personal life and/or the community, state, nation world that you live in today.

Once you have written out a list of ideas, please write a short explanation on why you selected what you did to place in the time capsule. (Note: It is not neces-

sary to write about each and every item. In fact, in order to make your piece as interesting as possible, select four or five items and go into some detail regarding your selection of each of them.) In focusing on the "why," be sure to discuss the importance of the item to you (personally and/or your local community or country in relation to the specific period of history in which you are living.

Reflection:

This quick write gets the juices flowing in students from the elementary to the university level. It's an ideal piece to use in a social studies or English class. It is also a quick write that can later be used by students as a starter to write fascinating essays or short stories.

Power of the Pen

Amy Young
Literacy Specialist,
OUR Educational Cooperative, Harrison, Arkansas

Directions:

The purpose of this activity is to get students to appreciate the power of writing to change the course of history. After a book study of *The Diary of Anne Frank* or a similarly well-written chronicle of "history in the making," ask students to consider the power of the written word upon society, governments, and the world as a whole. Ask students to make a list of as many written documents, books, letters, speeches, or memoirs that they feel have had a profound effect upon the people of the world or a nation. Allow about 3 minutes for this listing activity.

Examples students may cite include: Magna Carta, Mayflower Compact, Declaration of Independence, U.S. Constitution, Emancipation Proclamation, *Mein Kampf, Communist Manifesto, The Diary of Anne Frank*, Paul's letters to early Christian Churches, and so on.

Write suggestions from student lists on the board and allow a brief explanation of why each was chosen. Then ask students to choose the document/book, and so on, they deem most important to society or the world at large and write an explanation of their choice. Allow about 10 minutes.

Encourage students to share their pieces. Be sure to allow ample "wait time" between sharing.

Reflection:

This quick write can ideally be used near the end of the school year in a world or American history class. A key to its success is allowing students an opportunity to brainstorm the list and then select a topic of their choice from the list. Encourage students to defend their choice of topic with as much factual information as possible. The teacher may later want to ask students to expand their quick write into a persuasive or expository essay or a longer inquiry-based piece.

Radical Reactions

Samuel Totten
*Founder and Director of the Northwest Arkansas Writing Project
and Professor of Curriculum and Instruction,
University of Arkansas, Fayetteville*

Directions:

After handing out a copy of the Preamble to the U.S. Constitution to each student (but without a title or caption identifying the piece as the Preamble or being related to the Constitution), the teacher should read (*again, not identify the piece in any way whatsoever*) the Preamble to the U.S. Constitution aloud. The students should be asked to respond in writing to the ideas delineated in the piece. In doing so, they should be told, that they can note, for example, that they total approve of the ideas (noting why), adamantly disapprove (noting why), unconditionally accept (noting why), unconditionally reject (noting why), and/or note those sections they agree with or disagree with and why.

Once the students have responded in writing, the teacher should hold a class discussion (still not identifying the name or source of the piece) around the students' reactions. Once the discussion concludes, the teacher should reveal the fact that what the students have just responded to is the Preamble to the U.S. Constitution. A subsequent discussion should follow the revelation

Note: While this total activity (including the discussion) could take a full period or more, the writing, itself, *is* quick to do and constitutes the quick write.

Reflection:

This is an incredibly powerful introduction to the Preamble to the U.S. Constitution. Indeed, the discussion that results from this quick write is likely to be one of those school experiences that most students will never forget.

I'll Take You There

Becki Byrd
Director of Curriculum and Professional Development,
Greenwood School District, Greenwood, Arkansas

Directions:

Use Diane Siebert's books (*Sierra, Mississippi, Tour America*) or any other of your favorite authors who write well about "place" as frequent read alouds during a unit of study centered on regions, landforms, states, and so on. Keep a running list of interesting places, natural formations, and defining structures in the region posted on chart paper as instruction progresses.

At the end of the unit of study, briefly review and discuss the class list. Direct students to select one of the places from the list and write as many facts about the place as they can in 4 to 5 minutes. Encourage students to write quick phrases, incorporating strong verbs and descriptive language. Challenge the writers to "take the reader there" with the facts and language they choose. After calling time, ask students to look at the list of facts they wrote, go back and organize them (by numbering), strengthen or clarify phrases, add words and facts as needed, or delete items that won't fit the way they've organized their information. Allow another four to five minutes for quick revision. Offer an opportunity for authors to share.

Reflection:

Diane Siebert's word choice, imagery, and use of personification make the Mississippi River and Sierra Mountains come alive. She weaves history and science into her narrative poetry and possesses a gift for "taking the reader there." This quick write always creates mixed results. Some students truly don't come up with more than a list of facts, while others use this as a springboard for great polished pieces. Often the desire to polish a piece results in more research into the place of choice. At any rate, whether students go on to do more with the quick write or not, the sharing allows them to hear unit information repeated in a different venue, and they seem to like it.

Sample From a Study of Arkansas Rivers

The lower Ouachita River winds her way
   through an old resort city.
   Dams obstruct her passage and

she spreads her watery fingers into green hills.
  Lake Hamilton and Catherine boast power boats and
  sailing boats and million dollar views.
She glides past Arkadelphia
  and spills into the West Gulf Coastal Plain.
The Plain, the Timberlands, where hunters come
  from near and far to hunt for deer in piney woods.
Then on Miss Ouachita strolls to El Dorado,
  The roaring twenties oil boom town
  whose townsfolk slept to the beat
  of black gold pumping, ta-dock … ta-dock.
Before she slips across the southern border
  she meanders through the Felsenthal National Wildlife Refuge,
  creating habitat for migratory waterfowl
  and protecting endangered species.
Lady Ouachita serves her Arkansas children well.

NIMBY or Not in My Back Yard!

Samuel Totten
Founder and Director of the Northwest Arkansas Writing Project
and Professor of Curriculum and Instruction,
University of Arkansas, Fayetteville

Directions:

Say: *A relatively recent phenomenon is the so-called NIMBY (a person who doesn't want something ugly, noisy, or potentially (or actually) dangerous placed near his/her home or community). More specifically, NIMBY is an acronym for "Not In My Backyard." Among the many battles various NIMBYs have fought against are the placement of nuclear plants in their communities, major freeways close to their homes, the dumping of radioactive tailings near or in their town, etc. NIMBYs gain support by speaking up about an issue, circulating petitions, conducting surveys, and/or holding protests.*

What would cause you to become a NIMBY and why? Take 5 to 8 minutes and write from your prospective as a NIMBY that does not want that _____ in your "backyard."

Reflection:

This quick write is ideal for an interdisciplinary unit (social studies/science and/or geography) that meshes key social issues and scientific issues. I've used this quick write with the students in the Interdisciplinary Methods (Social Studies/English) course in the University of Arkansas, Fayette-ville's Master of Arts in Teaching Program as an example of how to mesh two or more disciplines in an easy but powerful manner.

Double Meanings

Helen Eaton
4th-Grade Teacher,
Holcomb Elementary School, Fayetteville, Arkansas

Directions:

After a unit of study or discussion involving environmental issues such as pollution, clear cutting, non-renewable resources, or nature conservation, read *The Lorax* by Dr. Seuss. *The Lorax* is a book about a Once-ler who discovers that he can make the fabulous thneeds out of the beautiful truffula trees. His family sets up a smoke-chugging factory for his thriving business. Unfortunately he chops all of the trees down and dumps all of his factory waste into the lakes. This is very bad news for the brown bar-ba-loots, the swomee-swans, and the humming fish. The little Lorax is the only one who speaks for the trees and the creatures who've lost their homes.

Say: *I am going to read you a book that may be familiar to you. I know you read or heard books by Dr. Seuss when you were younger. Why do little kids like his books so much?* The students will respond by saying that they're funny, they have silly pictures, or they rhyme. *Yes, they are fun and silly, but did you know that Theodore Geisel, Dr. Seuss, often wrote his books with a double meaning? Many of his books have a meaning much deeper than the story that is told with silly words and funny pictures. I want you to enjoy the story, but I want you to think. What serious message is Dr. Seuss really trying to convey?*

Read the book. Without allowing discussion, have the students put their thoughts on paper. If a little guidance is needed, ask a few questions before they begin to write. *What is the underlying theme of this story? How does it compare to what is happening in the world today? Who or what could the characters represent? What else does this story remind you of?*

After writing time is over, have students choose their favorite or best sentence. Allow them to share that sentence. Then have them choose their best or most powerful word and share that one word.

Samples From 4th Grade Student Work:

"The Lorax was sort of annoying yet cool at the same time."

"The Once-ler wouldn't leave everything alone because he was getting all that money."

"People should think before doing something that is bad."

"The Lorax reminds me of Martin Luther King Jr. I think that because he was speaking for the animals and the trees. Dr. King helped and fought for all people just like the Lorax did."

"In the story the fish can go out of the water and walk on dry land right beside the factory. In Lake Erie it's different because the fish just die."

"I think Dr. Seuss is telling us that we should treat nature with respect."

Reflection:

I used this quick write with my class after studying about the land and resources of the midwestern states. We had learned about the huge forests that once covered the states near the Great Lakes. We'd also learned about the factories surrounding the Great Lakes and the pollution problems caused by them. This book, which had always seemed fun to them as young children, suddenly became serious. The students were anxious to go to the library to check out other books by Dr. Seuss to figure out what other hidden messages they'd missed when they were little kids.

This quick write could be used for other social studies topics with different Dr. Seuss books. For example, *Yertle the Turtle* is not just a funny little turtle who wants to be boss of the pond no matter who he has to step on or hurt to be on top. This book could follow a discussion or unit of study about Hitler. (In early drafts, Yertle actually had a little black moustache!) *Horton Hatches a Who* might be a good choice to follow a study of the reconstruction period after World War II.

REFERENCE

Seuss, Dr. (1971). *The Lorax*. New York: Random House.

Dinner for Two

Jennifer Jennings Davis
English Teacher,
Van Buren High School, Van Buren, Arkansas

Directions:

Although more than 20 years have passed since the first publishing of Gregory Stock's *The Book of Questions,* it presents issues that prompt immediate ponderings into the human condition.

Many of the questions in the book make for thought-provoking writing prompts. This quick write centers on Question #48, which I have slightly edited for classroom use. To begin this quick write, engage your students with the following: *Silently think about this for a moment: who, of anybody in the world, would you like to meet?* (Pause for time to think, then ask for a few students to volunteer their selections.) *Now, let's suspend disbelief for a moment and think about this question: "Given the choice of anyone in the world, whom would you want as your dinner guest?" Before we start, you are going to want to think about and incorporate the following two points in your writing: (1) Why did you select this person? and (2) What topics would you want to discuss with this person and why? Pick up your pens and go!*

Reflection:

This quick write has quite a bit of flexibility for students, as their responses can range from serious and reflective to silly and humorous. Many times after introducing the topic but prior to writing, students will want to discuss some conditions regarding the dinner guests. For example, a student usually asks if the guest had to be from our present time period. The class discussed and agreed to completely suspend disbelief and agreed that the dinner guests could be dead or alive, from any time period. If preferred, the instructor could determine limitations and conditions in advance.

The Book of Questions is an excellent source for several quick writes; however, some questions delve into very personal aspects of life, making them inappropriate for classroom use. With this in mind, preview the book carefully.

REFERENCE

Stock, G. (1987). *The book of questions.* New York: Workman.

The Simple Life

Norma Prentiss
Literacy Coach,
Nelson-Wilks-Herron Elementary, Mountain Home, Arkansas

Directions:

Say: *Think about a willow tree. It is rooted in the ground. It bends when strong winds blow and does not break. It doesn't worry about yesterday or tomorrow. It does just what it was designed to do. The writer of this hymn was comparing his life to a willow tree.*

Introduce the song "*Willow Tree*" and play it for your students. It is a traditional Shaker hymn that speaks of being simple, humble and free.

Say: *This hymn was written over 200 years ago when life was very hard. Think about what we know about the life of the Pilgrims. Now think about your life. Do you think your life is simple and free like a willow tree?*

Willow Tree
(Traditional Shaker hymn)
Aubrey learned this from the singing of Kentucky minister and musician, Randy Wilson

I will bow and be simple
I will bow and be free
I will bow and be humble
Yea bend like the willow tree.

I will bow this is the token
I will wear the easy yoke
I will bow and be broken
Yea I'll fall upon the rock.

Let's take about 5 minutes to write our thoughts. Would you like to live during the time of the Pilgrims? Do you feel free, or do you feel like your life is too busy?
Do you have time to do the things you love to do?
Allow students time to share their reflections.

REFERENCES

Atwater-Donnelly. (YEAR?) *Like the willow tree*. Honolulu, HI: Rabbit Island Music.
Levine, K. (1996) *Keeping life simple: 7 guiding principles, 500 tips, and ideas*. North Adams, MA: Storey Communications.

Immigration and You

Lacinda Files
6th- & 7th-Grade Teacher,
J.O. Kelly Middle School, Springdale, Arkansas

Directions:

A unit of study on early immigration or Ellis Island should include Russell Freedman's excellent book, *Immigrant Kids*. The book tells us that between 1880 and 1920, 23 million immigrants arrived in the United States. They were mostly poor Europeans looking for a better life for their families. These families crossed the Atlantic Ocean packed into "dark, foul-smelling compartments" as steerage passengers (the cheapest way to travel) aboard overcrowded ships. Upon arrival to America, the immigrants saw the Statue of Liberty, a beacon of hope after their long, tedious journey. But their journey was only beginning. First they had to pass through Ellis Island, the nation's chief immigrant processing center at the time. People were herded through a series of narrow makeshift chutes; much like cattle is processed in slaughter houses. Along the way, families were inspected, poked, prodded, questioned and made to wait for hours before being released to begin their new life. Many people's names were changed to "Americanize" them.

Freedman's book contains many wonderful photos of immigrant families, but it is the pictures of the children that are so poignant. Excerpts from letters and journals offer eye-witness testimony to the many trials faced by those who braved the journey and made America their new home.

Many of our current students have traveled with their families to America to begin a new life in a new, unfamiliar country. They have not spent weeks or months in the hold of a ship, but some of their journeys were none-the-less perilous and dangerous.

Say: *I am going to read you several passages from* Immigrant Kids *by Russell Freedman. Please pay close attention to the photos I am going to show you. These are pictures of real children who came to America with their families between 1880 and 1920. Notice how they're dressed and the expressions on their faces*

Read several passages, including some of the journal excerpts and portions of letters. Ask the students to think about a journey they have made, especially one in which they were not sure where they would end up. Ask students to write about this journey. Their piece should include how they felt on the journey and some specifics about what happened.

After writing for several minutes, ask for volunteers to share their pieces. Some students may only wish to share a small portion of their piece.

Samples of Student Work:

"I remember the bright lights of a city."

"I stayed with a woman and her family until my mother came. It was a long time before my mother came."

"I came in the night. Out of Mexico. In a car with all my family. We had no food. We stayed with my uncle so my dad could work and get some money."

"I didn't want to leave Mexico. I still miss my family and friends. Our house there was very big. Here, our house is not so big."

"I once went on a trip with my family. My dad wouldn't tell us where we were going. It was a big surprise, he said. We drove all through the night and during the next day. If I had paid attention to the road signs I might have guessed where we were going. Anyway, I remember trying to stay awake, but I just couldn't. I heard my dad say, 'We're here!' When I opened my eyes, I saw a huge sign that said, 'Disney World.'"

Reflection:

I used this lesson last year when I taught literacy and worked with 5th-grade students. Along with Russell Freedman's book, the classroom teacher and I read *Esperanza Rising* by Pam Munoz Ryan aloud to the class. Esperanza and her mother are forced to leave Mexico after her corrupt uncles kill her father and burn down their home. Esperanza's journey is similar to many of those recounted in Freedman's book. After reading, reflecting and writing about both books, as well as discussing the current state of immigration, our students demonstrated a firm grasp of the material and produced many touching pieces of writing about their own immigration experiences.

REFERENCES

Freedman, R. (1980). *Immigrant kids*. New York: Puffin Books.

Ryan, P. M. (2000). *Esperanza rising*. New York: Scholastic Press.

Capturing the Essence of History: Writing Captions for Political Cartoons

Samuel Totten
*Founder and Director of the Northwest Arkansas Writing Project
and Professor of Curriculum and Instruction,
University of Arkansas, Fayetteville*

Directions:

Quickly share two or three different political cartoon with the students (all of which have captions). Point out to the students that the captions are succinct, exacting in what they aim at and say, and often times witty. Teachers should also talk about how political cartoons are also aimed at helping the reader gain a deeper understanding of an issue and/or to influence the thinking of readers.

Next, give each student in the class the same three political cartoons. minus the captions (written lines). (Ideally, the cartoons are related to an issue being discussed in class and/or something that would be of inherent interest to the students)

Have each student carefully examine each of the political cartoons and write a caption for each. Once that is completed, have the students exchange cartoons. Once the exchange has been made, each student should select one cartoon and briefly write a commentary on the similarities/differences between how he/she personally interpreted the cartoon versus the person he/she switched cartoons with. A short class discussion should follow

Reflection:

This quick write involves a lot of higher level thinking, analysis and synthesis. It also presses students to be succinct, exact, and creative in their writing. It is an excellent exercise for use in English and composition classes as well as social studies and history classes (where the emphasis should not only be on the interpretation of the political cartoon and writing of the caption but the use of political cartoons historically to inform and influence readers about critical issues facing society).

First Encounter

Amy Young
Literacy Specialist,
OUR Educational Cooperative, Harrison, Arkansas

Directions:

The purpose of this activity is to get students to consider the time of early European exploration in the United States from the viewpoint of the "explored." As students are studying the activities of early European explorers in the Americas, discuss with them the difficulties faced not only by the explorers themselves, but also the difficulties faced by the Native Americans who were being "explored." Ask students to consider what it might have been like for a Native American their age to have encountered the European explorers for the first time. Ask students to consider the following aspects of the explorers' visit as though they were a Native American young person:

- What do these strangers want?
- Where have they come from, and why are they here?
- Why do they dress so strangely and look so different from us?
- Are they indeed some sort of "god"?
- How will their coming affect me, my family, and the way we live?
- Are they going to stay? Will more of them come?

Ask students to write a letter or journal reflection from the viewpoint of a Native American young person. They should describe their thoughts, fears, and feelings regarding these strangers who have come to their land.

NOTE: Before making the writing assignment, the teacher may wish to read *Encounter*, a picture book by Jane Yolen, which narrates a Native American boy's (Taino) impressions of Columbus's landing on the shores of San Salvador. The book is based on historical records regarding Columbus's landing and treatment of Native American people living on the island. *Morning Girl* by Michael Dorris is a short children's chapter book which is also ideal with this quick write.

Reflection:

For far too many years, social studies in American schools was taught from the "God ordained, manifest destiny" point of view which ignored the native people living in the "explored" area. Little or no attention has been given to discussion of the adjustments Native Americans and others have had to make in order to accommodate the new culture being imposed upon them. This quick write affords students the opportunity to consider the exploration and activities of the European explorers from the view point of the "explored."

This quick write is appropriate for students of all ages who are studying European exploration of the world. Its basic premise—telling the story from the viewpoint of the "explored," or in some instances the "invaded"— could be applied to other circumstances, places, and time frames, such as, writing from the viewpoint of a native citizen about the involvement of foreign troops in peace keeping efforts in Afghanistan and Iraq.

An alternative activity would be to use this activity at Thanksgiving writing from the point of view of a Wampanoag at the time of the first Thanksgiving. *Guests*, a short chapter book by Michael Dorris, would be an appropriate literary accompaniment.

I, Too, Was There

Amy Young
Literacy Specialist,
OUR Educational Cooperative, Harrison, Arkansas

Directions:

The purpose of this activity is to get students to consider the lives of people/families who lived before them. Students have been studying the westward movement of the pioneers and life on the frontier; therefore, they should have considerable background information from which to pull.

Ask students to consider the people/families involved in the westward movement. Discuss the living conditions of the many families who had moved to the frontier. What would it have been like to share a one room cabin with your entire family? How would the food you ate be different from the food you eat today? Think of the difficulties associated with the isolation—no nearby town to buy supplies, only wagons and horses/mules for transportation.

Listen as I read a reflection to you written by an Arkansas author, Crescent Dragonwagon. The book is called *Home Place*. After I read it, I want you to choose an object from the box. (Provide an assortment of items which might be found around an old "home place" e.g., tarnished silverware, horse shoes, rusty nails, bolts, hair comb with missing teeth, marbles, pieces of broken dishes with no sharp edges, etc.)

Think about the person who may have owned or used the object. Write a reflection from that person's point of view. Share with us through your writing what the life, feelings, and living conditions of your character were as they lived during that long ago time.

Allow about ten minutes for writing and share. Students may choose to develop these pieces into "full blown" stories/reflections at a later date.

Reflection:

This activity promotes personalization of the pioneers and their daily lives that reading from an assigned text can never do. It helps students to realize that the facts they read about involved actual, "flesh and blood" people.

I have also used this activity to have students write from the point of view of the chosen object. They "tell the story" of the tarnished silver spoon—from its birth in the English silversmith's shop to its demise in the rubble of a forgotten "home place." This activity, too, can result in creative, thoughtful, well-written pieces that students enjoy sharing with others.

I Dream of Going to ...

Samuel Totten
Founder and Director of the Northwest Arkansas Writing Project and Professor of Curriculum and Instruction, University of Arkansas, Fayetteville

Directions:

Say: *There are people who love to travel so much that they actually make lists of their top 10 or 20 places they wish to visit before they die. My own list, which I wrote out about 30 years ago, included all of the following places: (1) Serengeti Plain in Tanzania where tens of thousands of wildebeests and other animals pass across during the annual migration; (2) The ancient and exotic suqs or market places in Morocco; (3) The ghats where the bodies of Hindus are burned on pyres along the Ganges River following their deaths; (4) Machu Pichhu, the ancient Mayan city high up in the Andes of Peru; (5) New Zealand; Paris, France; (6) Cambodia; Cairo, Egypt and the Great Pyramids; (7) Istanbul, Turkey, and New Orleans, Louisiana.*

Now I wish to have you make a short list—a minimum of five places—where you ardently desire to visit in the years ahead. It can be any place in the state, the United States, the world, or the universe. OK, you have 2 minutes to make the list."

Once the 2 minutes are up have each student select one place and write about why he/she wishes to visit that place. Instruct the students to be vivid in relating what they hope to see and experience.

Reflection:

This activity/quick write prompts students to think about geography in a new and engaging manner. It also introduces students to new and interesting places in the United States, and helps them to appreciate the diversity of locales in the United States. Finally, it provides the students with a personal connection to the subject of geography.

Civil Rights

Rita S. Caver
10th-Grade Advanced Placement United States History Teacher,
Fayetteville High School, Fayetteville, Arkansas

Directions:

During the introduction to the Civil Rights movement of the 1960s, read the book *Rosa* by Nikki Giovanni (ill. by Bryan Collier). After you have answered any questions students still have about the actions of Rosa Parks and the aftermath, have students do one of the following:

1. Think and write about an issue involving your rights (or those of others) where you might feel strongly enough to say "no." This might be at school, involve local, state and/or federal government, or any other place where individual or group rights might be trampled on. Describe the issue and how you might take a stand like Rosa Parks did.

2. Write about another historical figure who said "no" to encourage change. Explain why you believe this person was right or wrong in their actions. Describe what you might have done in their place.

(I play "Sister Rosa" by the Neville Brothers at some point in this process.)

Reflection:
   High school students always enjoy story-book time and in this case the story is excellent reinforcement of the historical facts. This is especially effective when an issue has arisen in school that the students want to talk about. Generally you will get a blend of students who write about historical figures and those who write about topical issues.

What If?

Samuel Totten
*Founder and Director of the Northwest Arkansas Writing Project
and Professor of Curriculum and Instruction,
University of Arkansas, Fayetteville*

Introduction
   Many students—and many adults across the globe for that matter—perceive historical events as a given. That is, they seem to think that the actions/activities/incidents leading up to historical events were inevitable. But the fact is, no historical event was inevitable. Each historical event was a culmination of thoughts, words, arguments, counter-arguments, actions and reactions by human beings. In other words, at some point in time, it was always possible that those words and actions that ended up becoming a historical event (e.g., the establishment of the United States as a republic; the freeing of slaves in the South; the assassination of Abraham Lincoln; the Great Depression of 1929; the Watergate Affair; the overthrow of Saddam Hussein which morphed into the Iraqi War) could have been altered in some minor or significant way and thus resulted in something entirely different with potentially and/or radically different results and ramifications.

Directions
   First, I simply provide the students with a series of "What If" questions (such questions need to be geared to the students' knowledge base, background, level of schooling):

* What if Arkansas had never become a state, and, instead, different parts of its land mass had been incorporated into, for example, Oklahoma, Texas and Missouri?
* What if Abraham Lincoln had been killed in 1862 instead of 1865?

- What if women had never been granted the right to vote in the United States?
- What if the Soviet Union had developed the atom bomb before the United States?
- What if the U.S. had never dropped the atom bombs on Hiroshima and Nagasaki?
- What if Martin Luther King Jr. had never been born?
- What if Al Gore had won the presidency of the United States in 2000 and not George W. Bush.
- What if the Twin Towers in New York City had never been attacked and destroyed by terrorists?

Next, I provide the students with one or two lines that "respond" to the "what if" questions. That is, I provide the students with succinct insights as to how history may have turned out somewhat, if not radically, different. For example, I show an overhead with each original statement and then an explanatory comment:

EXAMPLE: What if Abraham Lincoln had been killed in 1862 instead of 1865?

A Possible Outcome: Some historians believe that had Lincoln been killed in 1862 there is a better than even chance that there would have been a negotiated peace (versus a war, the Civil War) and that it would have resulted in a divided country up through today and that slavery would have continued for at least another generation.

Next, I have each student create a minimum of five "What If" statements of their own. Each statement must relate to either U.S. history or the historical events they recently studied or are currently studying in their current history course (be it world history, U.S. history, U.S. government, Arkansas history, or some other form of history).

Once the students have completed that task, I ask those who wish to share some of their "What If" statements to do so.

Finally, I require the students to select one of their statements and then think and write about all of the possible outcomes that might have ensued had that "What If" statement been a reality.

Reflection:
This quick write activity is an outstanding way to encourage and engage students in thinking about how history is made, how history could be different than it is, and the ramifications as to history-making and history itself. What the students come up with in the way of "What If" state-

ments is often quite thought-provoking. This quick write lends itself to fascinating and instructive discussions in class.

It is wise to have the students retain their "What If" statements for they can be used for future quick writes.

Just a Lookin' for a Home

Amy Young
Literacy Specialist,
OUR Educational Cooperative, Harrison, Arkansas

Directions:

The purpose of this activity is to get students to empathize with the plight of the many homeless children forced to go west on the orphan trains to find a new life. Acquaint students with the plight of many immigrant and poverty stricken families in large American cities between the mid-1850s and late 1920s. Discuss how language barriers and lack of education and skills prevented many parents from being able to adequately support their large families of children. Elaborate on the loss of parents through disease, accidents caused by unsafe working conditions, and premature death. Describe how these factors led to many children being orphaned long before they were old enough to support themselves.

As the orphanages became more and more crowded with homeless children, one solution used to cope with the problem were "orphan trains." Orphans were loaded onto trains with an adult in charge. As the trains traveled west, most of the orphans found homes in the small towns and on farms in the Midwest. Often they were separated from siblings and friends as they embarked upon new lives with total strangers.

Ask students to imagine what it would be like to be an orphan child heading West on the orphan train to find a new home.

Allow 10 minutes for writing. Encourage students to share their writing. Be sure to allow ample "wait time" between sharing.

Reflection:

Personalizing the events in American history through the use of quick writes or "diary journal entry" writing related to unit studies promotes a deeper understanding of the human experience during various eras of time. The orphan train "phenomenon" is an especially poignant piece of our patchwork design of the American experience quilt. Students may respond to this stimuli with the beginning of some powerful, emotional pieces.

Eve Bunting's *Train to Somewhere* is a wonderfully crafted picture book to share as a part of the orphan train study.

They Came Across the Sea

Amy Young
Literacy Specialist
OUR Educational Cooperative, Harrison, Arkansas

Directions:

The purpose of this activity is to get students to consider what it would be like to be an immigrant coming to the United States with no knowledge of the language. Display pictures of "immigrants" throughout American history if possible. Included in these pictures might be pictures of the Pilgrims, immigrants coming to Ellis Island in the late 1800s—early 1900s, Vietnamese "boat people," and immigrants from Mexico and Cuba.

Ask students if some of their ancestors were immigrants and how they think their ancestors might have felt coming to a foreign nation to make a new home. Discuss with them what it would be like for them to go to a country where they did not know anyone and did not understand the language. They should pretend that their parents decided to go to this different country in order to find work and make a new home for their family.

Ask students how they would feel as they entered a new school where they had no friends, and they could not understand the teachers or the other students. Allow students 10 minutes for writing.

Encourage students to share their writing. Be sure to allow ample "wait time" between sharing.

Reflection:

This quick write works well as an introduction to the study of immigration in American history. It would also work equally well at the conclusion of the study as students pull together the factual knowledge they have gained and incorporate the "human" element into it. This quick write could be expanded into a longer, more developed narrative or expository piece of writing if the teacher chooses to have the students do so.

A number of children's and young adult authors have written fictional accounts of the immigration of foreigners to America looking to find a better way of life. Some appropriate literature for this study include *The Lotus Seed* by Sherry Garland; *Jesse Came Across the Sea* by Amy Hest; *Molly's Pilgrim* by Barbara Cohen; *Nory Ryan's Song* by Patricia Reilly Giff; *Esperanza Rising* by Pam Munoz Ryan; *The Circuit* by Francisco Jimenez; and the fantasy/historical fiction rendering of *The Orphan of Ellis Island* by Elvira Woodruff.

A Knight's Tale

M. Darlene Montgomery
10th-, 11th-, & 12th-Grade English Teacher,
Northside High School, Fort Smith, Arkansas

Directions:

Rent, buy, download, or borrow a copy of the movie, *A Knight's Tale,* starring Heath Ledger from Columbia Pictures, Inc. If you use the DVD version, go to scene selection: scene 2. Select that and then rewind about 1 minute. If you use the VCR version, skip the first part and start as Heath Ledger is preparing to joust. The opening credits will be rolling, and you will hear Queen's song, "We Will Rock You." You will see the crowd acting like they are at a contemporary football game: singing the song, beating time on the rail, a girl dancing in the bleachers, shirtless bleacher creatures drunk and stupid, and an attempt at the wave. Even the king starts singing the song and tapping the rhythm. Play the clip from the crowd singing and beating time to the king mouthing the words to the song. You'll quit just as Heath (Sir Ector) puts his visor down and puts his horse to the gallop to start the joust.

Say: *Students, we have been studying the medieval period both in this class and in your history class, so now is a good time to tap all that new knowledge. I'm going to show you a video clip from* A Knight's Tale *twice. Please focus on the odd mixture of modern and medieval cultures used by the director, Brian Helgeland. You may wish to make note of unusual elements he uses to capture the mood.*

Show the clip twice, but refrain from pointing out anything. *Say: Now, you have 5 minutes to develop five specific questions about this clip you would like to ask Mr. Helgeland in an interview.* Time and wait 5 minutes.

Say: *Using one or two of your questions as a basis, pretend you are the director and formulate a reasoned response to your question(s). The thought process is more important than the grammar because you only have 5 minutes. Begin.*

Reflection:

My students are a very visual generation and are familiar with a huge selection of videos. They view video clips as a treat, although they are often frustrated that I will very seldom show an entire movie. Several years ago I discovered that my very visual students are not careful observers. They frequently grab only superficial plot elements and never go further. They tend to miss out on key elements that truly forward a plot or contain the intrinsic purpose of the director or writer. My students also lack experience in questioning the world around them or formulating serious open-ended questions for discussion. Their world tends to be fact-based and fairly cut and dried. They too frequently are so immersed in survival mode—jobs, transportation issues, divorce, pregnancy, moving constantly, enlistment—that they have no experience with higher level thinking. This quick write gives them an opportunity to start in their comfort zone and stretch a bit into higher level thinking. Also, when studying the medieval period, students wonder what all this "old dead guy" stuff has to do with them. This method is one of many I use to show them how much richer their world is when supported by a background of cultural and literary knowledge from those "old dead guys." It's also a way to prepare students for the question preparation/debate/discussion events that are a part of senior English and the business world.

REFERENCE

Helgeland, B. (Director). (2001). *A knight's tale* [Film]. Columbia Pictures

Food Often Makes the Place

Samuel Totten
*Founder and Director of the Northwest Arkansas Writing Project
and Professor of Curriculum and Instruction,
University of Arkansas, Fayetteville*

Directions:

Share the following with the students: Particular places—states, regions, and countries are often associated with particular foods. For example: Wisconsin is famous for its cheeses, Maine its lobsters, Louisiana its gumbo, Mexico its tamales and chili rellenos, Milwaukee its "brauts," England its shepherd pies and blood puddings, France its baguettes, Texas its Tex Mex dishes, the South its barbecue, Australia its vegemite and chiko rolls, Israel its falafels, Maryland its crabs and crabcakes, Vermont its maple syrup, Palm Springs its date malts, India its samosas, and Thailand its satays.

I want you to think about a special dish, dessert, meal, drink that you've had in the locale /place where the food, dish or drink either originated or for what it is widely known for. Describe the dish, drink, meal in a good amount of detail (let us smell it, see it, taste it, enjoy it), where you had it (at a picnic, a favorite aunt and uncles, on the beach, in a cafe, in a fancy restaurant), and relate if and how the surrounding and atmosphere added to the enjoyment of the food, dish, drink. Use vivid description—that is, provide the reader with the feel of the place, along with the smells, taste, sounds and texture of the food.

Reflection:

Students love sharing such quick writes with their peers, and their peers seem to genuinely enjoy hearing them for they frequently highlight places they have never been, and often food they've never experienced. The quick writes that result from this activity serve as natural segues to discussing the uniqueness of different places and different cultures as well as different ways of seeing and experiencing life. That is true whether all of the quick writes are about different parts of the United States or beyond.

"It's Out There Somewhere, But Who Knows Where and Who Really Cares?"

Samuel Totten
*Founder and Director of the Northwest Arkansas Writing Project
and Professor of Curriculum and Instruction,
University of Arkansas, Fayetteville*

Directions:

Say: *Time and again it is reported in polls and surveys that U.S. citizens have no idea where certain countries in the world are located. That is, it has been reported that many high school students are unable to name the country that borders the United States on its most southern border. Likewise, it has been reported that many adult citizens of the U.S. cannot name the continents in which certain countries are located (e.g., Afghanistan, Egypt, Iraq), let alone the exact place where certain countries are located on a map (Brazil, Israel, Iran, Venezuela). In fact, in the U.S. presidential election of 2008, Republican Vice Presidential Candidate Sarah Palin reportedly referred to the entire continent of Africa as a country.*

Say: *Please respond to this assertion, and in doing so take a stand in which you agree with or disagree with it: It doesn't really matter if one knows where a country, city, or capital is located. In addition to stating your position, you must provide a solid rationale/explanation for your position.*

Reflection:

This is quick write is useful to generate a discussion in a geography or social studies class in regard to the significance of geography, knowledge of the world and where various continents and countries are located, and whether there is really a need to have such knowledge.

War Is ...

Samuel Totten
*Founder and Director of the Northwest Arkansas Writing Project
and Professor of Curriculum and Instruction,
University of Arkansas, Fayetteville*

Directions:

The teacher should read the students one of three pieces about war: Mark Twain's "War Prayer"; Stephen Crane's "War is Kind" or Wilfred Owen's, "Dulce et Decorum Est Pro Patria Mori."

Inform the students that they will have 10 minutes to write a rough draft of a piece on how they feel about war. It is critical to inform the students that they can take any slant they wish: patriotic; satirical; a parody of Twain, Crane, Owen, and so on. The key, tell them, is that the piece they write should be written from the heart and the mind, be pungent, and, hopefully, get people thinking in a different way about war.

Reflection:

This quick write is often extremely thought-provoking for it results in many pieces that are extremely diverse in perspective and tone. It is an ideal activity to use when reading literature (poetry, short stories or novels) that deal with war and/or during a discussion of a particular war in a social studies/history class.

The Most Perfect Place in the Universe

Samuel Totten
*Founder and Director of the Northwest Arkansas Writing Project
and Professor of Curriculum and Instruction,
University of Arkansas, Fayetteville*

Part (or Day) 1

Teachers should share the following with his/her students:

The term "utopia' literally means "no place." In common parlance, though, it means a place of perfection—where everything is ideal. That said, over the past several centuries many authors have created literary works around the idea of "utopias" or a perfect world.

When one thinks about it, we all probably have our own conception of what a perfect world would look like and consist of. Each of our utopias would likely be quite different for we each have different belief systems, hopes, aspirations, goals, and dreams.

In the next 5 minutes I want you to simply list all of the components/aspects that would go into the development of your very own utopia. You do not need to use complete sentences for this exercise. Indeed, single words or phrase are just fine. That said, if you wish to use complete sentences then please do so.

Once the students have completed their lists, any who wishes to share can be asked to do so.

Ask the students to place their names on their lists and to hand them in. Tell them that tomorrow, or later in the week, the lists will be handed back out and be used for another quick write exercise.

Part (or Day) 2

After returning each student's list, the teacher should tell the students the following: *OK, using the list of components/aspects you developed in regard to what you would want to include in your own utopia, I want you to create, in a paragraph or two, both a description of your utopia and a rationale as to why you would create such an utopia (that is, why such components are so important to the utopia you would create). You have 5 to 10 minutes to write a rough draft.*

Ask the students to place both the original list and the draft in their portfolios. Tell them this is another piece that they may wish to return to in the future.

Reflection:

This quick write is an excellent anticipatory set to use in a social studies, government or literature class in preparation to discuss the concepts of utopia and/or dystopia.

Civil Disobedience

Samuel Totten
*Founder and Director of the Northwest Arkansas Writing Project
and Professor of Curriculum and Instruction,
University of Arkansas, Fayetteville*

Directions:

Teachers should inform their students of the following: *Over the past 150 years or so, many citizens in the United States and across the globe have committed civil disobedience in order to protest situations that they've perceived as being unfair, illegal or corrupt. Simply stated, "civil disobedience" is the nonviolent refusal by an individual or group of people to obey governmental practices (including laws) as a way of forcing concessions from the government. Some of the most famous civil disobedients have been Henry David Thoreau, who refused to pay taxes to the U.S. government because he thought the government was wrong in carrying out the Mexican-American War and he did not want his tax money going to the war effort; the suffragists at the turn of the twentieth century who fought for the women's right to vote in the United States; Mahatma Gandhi, who used and encouraged the people of India to use civil disobedience to free India from British oppression; Rosa Parks, a black woman who helped to spark the civil rights movement in the United States by refusing to relinquish her seat on a bus to a white man; and Daniel and Philip Berrigan, two Catholic priests, who protested, among other concerns, the United States' involvement in the Vietnam war, and the nuclear arms race.*

I wish to have you approach this quick write in one of two ways. First, you may discuss an issue that you would be willing to commit civil disobedience over and why, or second, you can respond to whether you think civil disobedience is a good idea or a bad idea and why.

Reflection:

This is a perfect quick write with which to either (1) introduce the concept of civil disobedience, (2) use during a study of Henry David Thoreau's "On Civil Disobedience" or Martin Luther King, Jr's "Letter from a Birmingham Jail," (3) or any act of civil disobedience (e.g., the Boston Tea Party, the antinuclear power and weapons protests of the 1989s, the antiapartheid protests, the ongoing genocide in Darfur, Sudan).

I'd Like to Get to Know You

Samuel Totten
**Founder and Director of the Northwest Arkansas Writing Project
and Professor of Curriculum and Instruction,
University of Arkansas, Fayetteville**

Directions:

The teacher should say: *On Sunday, many local newspapers run a story about a local person who has accomplished something special and/or has a unique story. Oftentimes when the local person is interviewed, he or she is asked which famous person(s) would he/she most like to meet (or a variant is, have dinner with) and why.*

I often find myself answering such a question myself and among those I have noted are the following (individual teachers should insert their own list herein): American novelist Ernest Hemingway; Greek novelist Nikos Kazantzakis; the muckraking journalist Jack Anderson; Henry David Thoreau; the Berrigan brothers, the two noted Catholic priests who were anti--war and ant-nuclear activists; Andrei Shakarov, the famous Russian physicist and dissident; Gandhi; Martin Luther King, Jr.; Linus Pauling, two time Nobel Prize Winner; Nelson Mandela; Sylvia Beach, owner of the famous bookstore, Shakespeare and Company, in Paris during the 1920s and 1930s, among many others.

I wish to have you write out your own list—five to ten individuals will suffice. Once you've completed your list to your satisfaction, select one person and state why you would greatly enjoy meeting and getting to know that person.

Reflection:

This quick write is ideal for use in English, social studies and/or science class. It is a good way to get students thinking about those people have made a mark in the world for one reason or another. It is also a good way to encourage students to learn more about the individual they've written about, whether its through reading an autobiography, biography or something on the internet about the person.

One Wish to Make the World a Better Place

Samuel Totten
*Founder and Director of the Northwest Arkansas Writing Project
and Professor of Curriculum and Instruction,
University of Arkansas, Fayetteville*

Directions:

Say: *More and more often today, extremely wealthy people are using their millions and billions of dollars to help the world become a better place. For example, Bill Gates, one of the founders of Microsoft, has provided numerous African countries tens of millions of dollars with various types of assistance in order to the HIV/ AIDS epidemic, to develop and grow new strains of crops to help offset a lack of adequate quantities of food where people go hungry everyday, and in other ways.*

One, though, does not have to have mounds of money to help make the world a better place. In fact, one thing that is needed is an abundance of original and good ideas. For example, many young people—from junior high age through college—have come up with valuable ways to help others in the world. For example, a group of young students living near San Jose, California, created the African Water Project. During their first 2 years, the students raised more than $12,000, to be used for bringing safe drinking water to various communities throughout Kenya and Zambia. The funds have supported the drilling of three new wells and the repair of others. (Teachers may wish to go on line in order to locate two or three other stories of young people making a difference in different ways.)

In that vein, and in the next 5 minutes, as a class, let's brainstorm all of the different ideas we can come up with that could help make the world a better place. (Hold the brainstorming session for several minutes.)

Okay, now I wish to have you select one of the ideas on the overhead, or another idea you have in your head, and discuss why and how the idea/project would truly make the world a better place.

Reflection:

This is a good quick write to use with students in a community service course or a social studies class. If nothing else, it prods and encourages students to think of others beside themselves and how they might, either in a some small and important way today—or even bigger way down the road when they are older—reach out to help others who are less fortunate than themselves or to come up with a way to make the world a better place for everyone.

Printed in the United States
214274BV00002B/4/P